AFTER JESUS, EVERYTHING ELSE IS
HARDLY WORTH TALKING ABOUT

IT'S ALL ABOUT *Him*

To order additional copies of *It's All About Him* by Lee Venden, call 1-800-765-6955.

Visit us at www.reviewandherald.com for information on other Review and Herald® products.

AFTER JESUS, EVERYTHING ELSE IS
HARDLY WORTH TALKING ABOUT

IT'S ALL ABOUT

Him

LEE VENDEN

REVIEW AND HERALD® PUBLISHING ASSOCIATION
HAGERSTOWN, MD 21740

The author assumes full responsibility for the accuracy of all facts and quotations as cited
in this book.

Bible texts credited to Amplified are from *The Amplified Bible,* Old Testament copyright
© 1965, 1987 by the Zondervan Corporation. *The Amplified New Testament* copyright © 1958,
1987 by The Lockman Foundation. Used by permission.

Texts credited to Message are from *The Message.* Copyright © 1993, 1994, 1995, 1996,
2000, 2001, 2002. Used by permission of NavPress Publishing Group.

Texts credited to NIV are from the *Holy Bible, New International Version.* Copyright © 1973,
1978, 1984, International Bible Society. Used by permission of Zondervan Bible Publishers.

Texts credited to NKJV are from The New King James Version. Copyright © 1979,
1980, 1982 by Thomas Nelson, Inc. Used by permission. All rights reserved.

Bible texts credited to NRSV are from the New Revised Standard Version of the Bible,
copyright © 1989 by the Division of Christian Education of the National Council of the
Churches of Christ in the U.S.A. Used by permission.

Bible texts credited to RSV are from the Revised Standard Version of the Bible, copyright © 1946, 1952, 1971, by the Division of Christian Education of the National Council of
the Churches of Christ in the U.S.A. Used by permission.

Verses marked TLB are taken from *The Living Bible,* copyright © 1971 by Tyndale
House Publishers, Wheaton, Ill. Used by permission.

This book was
Edited by Andy Nash
Copyedited by James Cavil
Designed by Freshcut Design
Cover art by Lars Justinen
Typeset: Bembo 12/14

PRINTED IN U.S.A.

08 07 06 05   5 4 3

R&H Cataloging Service
Venden, Lee, 1955-
    It's all about Him

    1. Christian life.   I. Title.

        248.8

ISBN 0-8280-1807-3

This book is dedicated to

MARJI,

my life companion
whose consistent example
of turning to God
as readily as the flower
turns toward the sun,
is an ongoing inspiration to me.

"There are many fine women in the world,
but you are the best of them all!
A woman who fears and reverences God
Shall be greatly praised."
—*Proverbs 31:28-30.*

Contents

Introduction

*H*ave you ever wondered how to *really* give God your heart, surrender your will, develop a personal relationship with Jesus, be born again? It is one thing to know the terms, the theology, and the rules (information *about* God), but it can be an altogether different thing to actually *know* God.

It's All About Him is a book on how to get to know Jesus. It shows you how a personal relationship with Jesus is the sum and substance of the Christian life. More than that, it offers tangible, practical, plain-English suggestions on how to develop and/or maintain a *meaningful* friendship with Jesus. It is a hands-on book that addresses the nuts and bolts, the nitty-gritty, of developing a meaningful devotional life and ministry with Christ.

Chapter 1: Love relationships always involve two people. This chapter considers a personal relationship between God and you—from God's point of view. Not Do you need God? but Does God need you?

Chapter 2: The case from Scripture that Christianity, at its core, is not about what you do, but who you know.

Chapter 3: The need for conversion and how to experience it.

Chapter 4: A practical recipe for experiencing a meaningful devotional life as one of the key ingredients in a personal relationship with God.

Chapter 5: How prayer is not dialing 911 but primarily communion with God. Also, practical suggestions on how to experience two-way communion when talking with Him.

Chapter 6: Why sharing Jesus with others is essential to maintaining a personal relationship with God. How the Christian witness benefits God, others, and you. What witness is, and what it is not, and how to be an effective witness.

Chapter 7: How to deal with one of Satan's most effective weapons—discouragement over personal failure and apparent lack of spiritual growth. How Jesus fights *for* us and our part in overcoming.

Chapter 8: The matchless friendship of Jesus and how He provides for every need of ours.

Chapter 9: Jesus is not only personally interested in each one of us, but He is the same yesterday, today, and forever.

A little girl once wrote C. S. Lewis telling how she loved his *Narnia* series. She mentioned having a particular fondness for Aslan (the lion) because he reminded her so much of Jesus—whom she loved dearly. She then went on to say that she had tried reading some of Lewis's theological works and had gotten quite bogged down. She concluded by asking him if he could help clear up some of her confusion regarding those books.

Scholar, writer, and professor though he was, Lewis took the time to reply to the young girl. After telling her how pleased he was to know that she loved Jesus, he told her not to worry about understanding the other books. "Because," he concluded, "as long as Jesus is your friend, I am certain that nothing too bad will ever happen to you."

We can be friends with God. He is coming back for His friends, and He has made Himself *responsible* for seeing that we're ready to go home with Him. With a friend like that, it's not difficult to see how even the worst circumstances will ultimately have a happy ending. What a friend we have in Jesus!

CHAPTER 1

No Other Message

A few years ago I attended a concert given by Michael Card, a Christian songwriter and musician that I consider noteworthy (no pun intended) because of his steady focus on Jesus. Perhaps my favorite work of his is entitled *The Life,* a two-album set on the life of Jesus from the cradle to His final coronation. At the concert Card came on stage and played his first song—which was about Jesus. When he finished that song, he told the audience, "All of the songs are going to be about Him tonight. There is really no one else worth singing about." His conclusion reminds me of Colossians 1:16-23, as paraphrased by Eugene Peterson in *The Message.*

"Everything, absolutely everything, above and below, visible and invisible, rank after rank after rank of angels—*everything* got started in him and finds its purpose in him. He was there before any of it came into existence and holds it all together right up to this moment. . . . . He was supreme in the beginning and—leading the resurrection parade—he is supreme in the end. From beginning to end he's there, towering far above everything, everyone. So spacious is he, so roomy, that everything of God finds its proper place in him without crowding. Not only that, but all the broken and dislocated pieces of the universe—people and things, animals and atoms—get properly fixed and fit together in vibrant harmonies, all because of his death. . . . By giving himself completely at the Cross, actually *dying* for you, Christ brought you over to God's side. . . . You don't walk away from a gift like that! You stay grounded and steady in that bond of trust, constantly tuned in to the Message [Christ], careful not to be distracted or diverted. There is no other Message—just this one. Every creature under heaven gets this same Message."

There is no other message, just this one. It's all about Him! It starts with Him, it ends with Him, and He is everything in between. Jesus, Jesus, Jesus! That's why I like the song "More About Jesus."

> "More about Jesus I would know,
>   More of His grace to others show;
>   More of His saving fullness see,
>   More of His love who died for me.
>   More, more about Jesus,
>   More, more about Jesus;
>   More of His saving fullness see,
>   More of His love who died for me."

It's all about Him! There is no other message, just this one. Jesus! Only Jesus! It reminds me of a bumper sticker: "After Alaska, everything else just looks like Texas." It inspires me to say, "After Jesus, everything else is hardly worth talking about!" It's all about Him, and it keeps coming back to this one thing: Jesus and His Father just want to be friends with you and me. In fact, the Old Testament and the New Testament could fairly accurately be boiled down to one question: God asking "Can we be friends?"

That was His plan from the beginning; that's why He created Adam and Eve. He wanted to enlarge His family circle for love and friendship. Unfortunately, Adam and Eve thought it best to "break up." When I was younger, guys and girls who were romantically involved were referred to as "going steady." Then, if the romance ended, it was known as "breaking up." Adam and Eve decided it would be best if they "broke up" with God.

Breaking Up Is Hard to Do

Has anybody ever broken up with you? How did it feel? I can remember my first girlfriend. Kathy and I became special friends toward the end of eighth grade. An evangelist came to our town to present a series of meetings in a local church, and Kathy asked her parents if they would drop her off to attend those meetings. I asked my parents the same thing (our parents were delighted we had such an interest in attending religious meetings). And those were *wonderful* meetings!

I remember sitting at the back of the church in a room intended for parents of small, restless children. It had a glass window that looked into the sanctuary, and a speaker that piped in the sound, but it was really quite private. Kathy and I sat side by side on folding metal chairs in this dimly lit room. Music played as a chalk artist did a special drawing at the front of the church, which he showed off under black light as he completed it. The main house lights were dimmed in order for the audience to get the full effect of the black-lit picture, and it was during those magic moments that my right hand bumped into Kathy's left hand. Before either of us quite knew how it happened, we found ourselves holding hands. I'll never forget the electrical charge that raced from my neck down my spine as we touched! I had no idea that holding a girl's hand could do such a thing to a guy! Oh, those were wonderful meetings! I think we made it to every one in the series.

We finished off our eighth-grade year and continued our romance through the summer. Kathy had an Old English sheepdog, and when I'd visit we took it for walks in her neighborhood. We both had Honda 90 motorcycles but were not old enough to ride them on the street, so our parents would take us to high school parking lots where we would ride together. Romance!

But summer ended, and so did our romance as we arrived in high school and I watched Kathy walk off into the sunset with Jim Bargas. I don't remember very many names from that school year, but I remember Jim Bargas! He was a tall sophomore who had a driver's license and his own car. Heartbreak! I hadn't known romance could send a shock down your spine, nor did I know that it could fracture your heart as well.

I was so deeply hurt over that breakup that it was two years before I had courage enough to pursue romance. This time the relationship lasted nearly two years, with an ending that caught me by surprise. One

Friday evening I noticed Greg's car in front of Lori's house as I came to visit. I naively assumed that he was there to visit one of Lori's three sisters. Shortly after I arrived, however, Greg said good night and left me alone with Lori, who snuggled up to me and said, ever so tenderly, "I think that it would be best if we were *just* friends."

When a girl tells a guy that she just wants to be friends, he needs to understand that what she means is: "Please don't come to see me anymore, don't call me, don't write me, don't send me gifts or flowers, don't hang around with my friends, don't talk to me at school . . . because I *just* want to be friends."

I went home that night so devastated that instead of going to bed, I went into my parents' room and stood beside their bed until my mother woke up and asked me what was wrong. Tearfully I told her that Lori had just broken up with me and that I didn't know what I was going to do. As I stood there, broken, in the darkness, my mother gently and tenderly comforted me with these words: "Lee, there are *other* fish in the sea." Would you have felt comforted by that? I wasn't even a fisherman, and I had no interest in the sea.

Heartbroken! I remember going to the library to study for a test and being unable to concentrate because I kept remembering the times I had studied there with Lori. I tried going for a drive, but I was ambushed by the memory of Lori riding in the passenger seat. I thought perhaps a walk in the forest might help, but found myself remembering similar walks with Lori. Breaking up is devastating!

I tried to win her back with a poem and a flower. I still remember the last stanza in the poem:

> So goodbye,
>> but before I finally depart,
> Let me tell you,
>> you still have a piece of my heart.
> It's only a piece,
>> just a small little token,
> But pieces don't happen
>> unless things get broken.

If you had been Lori, would you have given me another chance after that poem? Lori didn't, but I can tell you now that I am glad she didn't . . . because Marji *did*. Twenty-five years later Marji's still with me, and I'm convinced that God knew what He was doing when He blessed me with her!

Feeling Rejection

Philip Yancey, the author of *The Jesus I Never Knew* and *Where Is God When It Hurts?* tells about going to the Rocky Mountains of Colorado to spend two weeks in a cabin with no company but his Bible. He went there for the specific purpose of reading all the way through the Bible quickly, to try to get a bird's-eye view of the Scriptures. He wanted to see what recurring themes would surface while reading in that manner. He tells of being struck with the conclusion that the entire Bible could be boiled down to *one effort after another of God's seeking a restored relationship with human beings.*

Adam and Eve broke up with God, and the entire Bible is an account of God's seeking time after time, way after way, century after century, to have a restored relationship with us. "Can we be friends?" Think about *God* feeling rejected for 6,000 years! There is no other message, just this one: "Can we be friends?"

Have you ever been rejected? Maybe it was a job you really wanted but didn't get. Maybe a fiancé broke the engagement, and you never reached the wedding chapel. Maybe a spouse asked you for a divorce. Maybe you are the child of a divided home, and you just aren't sure whether either parent really wants you around. How does it feel? Do you remember?

Maybe you can remember being chosen last for games during school recess—one captain told the other team that they could pick two players if they chose you. Maybe you can remember being nominated for a class office, leaving the room during the vote, and then coming back in to discover that someone else had won the election. Maybe you offered to do a favor or kindness for someone that wasn't accepted or appreciated. Do you remember how it felt?

Maybe you can remember *not* attending a banquet or prom that your other friends attended. Maybe you weren't invited, or maybe no one accepted your invitation. Maybe you auditioned for a music group and didn't make it. Do you remember feeling naked, exposed, vulnerable, and rejected? How did it feel to be passed over? How did it feel to be considered undesirable, unincluded, unwanted?

The Vulnerability of God

In John 13 Jesus tells Peter he is going to deny Him. In Matthew 26 you can read the account of how Peter *did deny* Jesus. Then in John 21, after the Resurrection, by the Sea of Galilee, Jesus asks Peter a question three times. Do you remember the question? "Peter," He says, "Do you love Me?" And again . . . and again. What is going on here?

Do you realize how vulnerable that question is? When you ask somebody if they love you, you are sticking your neck out. That's why the schoolchildren ask a *friend* to ask that special someone "if they like me." Why? Because they can't face the possibility of rejection in person. It's a scary thing to ask somebody if they like you!

The Creator and God of the universe is asking if we care about Him. The Jesus who died a bloody, godforsaken death that we might live is asking if we love Him! The vulnerability of God in permitting Himself to be affected by our response! It almost takes your breath away.

The heartbreak of Jesus as He wept over Jerusalem for not receiving Him: "O Jerusalem, Jerusalem, how I have longed to gather you as a hen gathers her chicks, but you would not" (see Matthew 23:37). As you study that story, you discover that these were not silent tears that quietly slipped down Christ's cheeks for a moment or two. His whole body shook as with a tempest, His chest heaved, and wails burst from His breaking heart. Those around Him began to weep in sympathy with a grief they could not comprehend.

The vulnerability of God: "Do you love Me?" "O Jerusalem!" This is utterly astounding!

Brennan Manning, in his book *Abba's Child,* says, "That there was no room in the inn was symbolic of what was to happen to Jesus. The only place there was room for Him was on a cross. He sought an entry to the overcrowded hearts of men; He could not find it, and still His search continues and His rejection goes on."

Consider Isaiah 53 as written in the present tense: "He *is* despised and rejected of men; a man of sorrows, *still* acquainted with grief: and we *hide* as it were our faces from him; he *is* despised still, and we *esteem* him not" (see verse 3).

"Surely he took up our infirmities and carried our sorrows, yet we considered him stricken by God, smitten by him, and afflicted. But he was pierced for our transgressions [can we be friends? do you love Me?], he was crushed for our iniquities; the punishment that brought us peace was upon him, and by his wounds we are healed [can we be friends?]" (verses 4, 5, NIV).

"He was oppressed and afflicted, yet he did not open his mouth; he was led like a lamb to the slaughter, and as a sheep before her shearers is silent, so he did not open his mouth. [Can you see His pleading eyes? Can we be friends?] By oppression and judgment he was taken away. [Can you see Him looking back over His shoulder into your eyes . . . *would* you love Me?] And who can speak of his descendants? For he was cut off from the land of the living; for the transgression of my people he was stricken. He was assigned a grave with the wicked, and with the rich in his death, though he had done no violence, nor was any deceit in his mouth [can we be friends?]" (verses 7-9, NIV).

It isn't *Do you need God?* That's the way we usually approach the question. We talk about why we need God, why we ought to make a decision for God, why it would be in our best interests to choose God. But let's turn the table. Let's consider it from a different perspective. *Does God need you?* One page after another in the Bible describes God seeking to restore a broken relationship because He loves you.

Does God need you? Sometimes we end our prayers by saying, "For Jesus' sake, amen." Isn't it time we responded to Heaven's invitation for friendship, *for Jesus' sake?* That's right: for Christ's sake! Can we be friends?

Looking Through the Parent Window

Parents understand this concept to some degree as they think about their children. Why do couples choose to have children? To

get another tax deduction? I don't think so. For all the extra help
with household chores? Hardly! Most parents choose to have children to increase the circle of love within their home. Our children
are precious because of the love, warmth, and affection they bring
to our hearts.

I've known parents who looked forward to the day when their
children would leave the nest and they could have the house to
themselves again. But that's not the way I think. "Watercolor
Ponies," "Butterfly Kisses," and "Sunrise, Sunset" reduce me to tears
every time I hear the songs. For Marji and me, the thought of our
children leaving home fills our hearts with sadness. It's not "Do they
need us?" *We need them!*

When my 19-year-old son graduated from high school, I knew
he would be home only a few more weeks before he headed off to
college. When he left, he'd be leaving for good. It would never be
the same again. He would go off to college and come home for holidays. Eventually he would start missing some of the holidays, because he will be going to a sweetheart's home instead. And then they
will have a home, and we will see them only now and then. It will
never be the same once they go off to college. Now I can understand more fully why my mom wrote me the following letter so
many years ago.

December 3, 1974
370 Cold Springs Road
Angwin, California

Dear Lee,

How do you write to your firstborn son who is on his
first real solo flight? You put it off because somehow he
seems older than you are. It's past the time for maternal advice because he already knows almost everything about what
you think pertaining to him—but he doesn't know the pain
around his mother's heart as she watches him leave to become a man.

Experience is the best teacher, so they say, but you can't

learn from our experience, because it is not the same as finding out for yourself. Your mom wishes she could be there to pick you up if you fall and encourage you to try again the way she did when you learned to walk. She wishes she could be there to tell you that you *are* missed and that you *will be* missed. To say that doesn't really say what I would like to say, but you *are* missed and you *will be*.

I miss seeing the awful mess all over the basement. Daddy put it in order today, and now it looks cold and unfriendly in a sterile sort of way. I guess I didn't prepare myself for your leaving like I should have. I just wouldn't think about it, but maybe you can't really think about it until it happens.

I'm grateful to God for having you as a son and that you put up with us for these 19 years. I hope you won't stop putting up with us. I wanted to write something really poetic or heavy, but the words just won't come. This is not intended to make you homesick or to get you to come home. This is really just therapy for your mother. I want you to know that I love you . . . more than just saying "I love you" as you went out the door. I miss you, but I'm glad for your opportunity to grow and mature. I'm proud of you and appreciate the *friend* you were to me.

I'm not sure that I will mail this letter, but it has been good for me to write my feelings and even to shed a few tears. Keep in touch, Lee. We need it more than you do.

Your loving mother.

At-one-ment

Can we be friends? Peter, do you love Me? For Christ's sake, for God's sake, for Jesus' sake, can we be friends?

"Look! I have been standing at the door and I am constantly knocking. If anyone hears me calling him and opens the door, I will come in and fellowship with him" (Revelation 3:20, TLB). Can we be friends? He knocks *every morning!* He had just finished serving breakfast the morning He asked Peter, "Do you love Me?" He still serves breakfast every morning. It's called the devotional life—taking some time alone with God at the beginning of the day for the purpose of knowing Him better. How do you respond when He knocks?

His heart is out on a platter. He is not ashamed to beg you, "Can we be friends? Do you love Me?" He stretched His arms on a wooden cross to show you how much He wants at-one-ment. Example after example of God's seeking to restore a broken relationship with human beings. "You stay grounded and steady in that bond of trust, constantly tuned in to [Jesus], careful not to be distracted or diverted. There is no other Message—just this one" (Colossians 1:22, 23, Message).

Have You Ever?

Do you know what it's like to be lonely? to be so alone that your own thoughts are your only companions? Do you know what it's like as a child to want to play with other children and meet only ridicule?

Do you know what it's like to wish for a retreat in the quiet of your own home, but even there find laughter and sarcasm? Do you know what it's like to spend hours, days, and nights in the lonely refuge of mountain or desert? Do you know what it's like to sit high on a lonely mountain overlooking a city, wishing you could be someone's friend? Do you know how it feels to sleep on rough ground without a blanket year after year?

Have you ever walked through a crowd, attended a dinner party, or passed through a marketplace teeming with people, yet somehow still felt alone? Have you ever watched from the shadows while others enjoyed an activity or game? Have you ever been invited by someone to get acquainted and then been asked to come after dark so no one would glimpse you together?

Have you ever fed a large crowd and discovered that the food that you provided was more appreciated than you were?

Have you ever walked for days along a hot, dusty highway and finally reached a town, only to be asked to leave?

Have you ever walked 30 miles to comfort a bereaved family, only to be treated as if it were *your* fault the sick person had died?

Have you ever been turned away no matter where you went or whom you asked for lodging?

Have you ever returned to your hometown acquaintances seeking to give friendship, and had rocks thrown at you? Do you know how it hurts to have no one to talk to, no one to share with, even if that person would only listen?

Have you ever cried so hard that your eyes ached and, trying to talk, you could only moan between sobs? Have you ever spent nights in tears that no one will ever know of except you?

Have you ever thought that you had found a few who accepted you as their friend and then watched as they left or ignored you so as not to be embarrassed by you? Have you ever felt the pain of rejection or the bitter disappointment of broken trust? Have you ever given of yourself till there was nothing left to give and then heard mocking laughter because you were so vulnerable?

Have you ever sat alone by the edge of a lake and watched gulls drift above the water, wishing you could fly away? Have you ever struggled against giving up the effort to give yourself, struggled until you actually sweat blood?

Have you ever spent entire nights worrying and praying for a troubled friend? Have you gone to that same friend and heard him say, "I'm too tired to listen"?

Have you ever had people follow you everywhere so that they might distort something you say and justify putting you to death? Have you ever been rudely jostled by calloused men, helpless within their menacing circle, because of love? Have you ever had someone spit upon your bruised and bleeding face? Have you ever felt blood trickling down your back from torn flesh while being beaten by a leather whip with metal strips attached to it?

Have you ever felt the sharp pain of thorns forcefully pressed deep into your scalp and temples? Have you ever had to wipe your eyes with a blood-sopped sleeve in order to see through tears? Do you know how it feels to struggle through your own blood while dragging heavy timbers? Do you think you could stagger on, willingly, dying for those who hate, despise, and reject you? Would you bear screaming insults, laughter, and mocking as you collapsed beneath your instrument of death? Would you struggle desperately to rise and continue toward your place of execution?

Have you ever felt the tearing, grinding, crunch of nails being pounded through your hands and feet? Have you ever felt, with every nerve, the jolting thud of a cross dropped into its deeply dug hole? Have you ever hung from nails, with open wounds gaping ever wider while crowds taunted, throwing rocks at your bruised and lacerated body? Have you ever hung outstretched as rain and wind buffeted your exhausted body against a cross?

Have you ever gasped hoarsely for breath, aware that you are dying? Do you know how it feels to have vision grow dim as your eyes glaze? Have you ever exhaled your last breath, knowing it is finished?

Have you ever hurt? Have you ever ached? Have you ever suffered? Have you ever died—alone—for people who refused to let you be their friend?

While on earth, Jesus longed for companionship. He still does. Will you be His friend?

For Further Reflection

1. Read the following passages describing Jesus, and ask yourself how much of what you need is found in Him. Proverbs 3:6; Isaiah 9:6; Isaiah 26:3; Matthew 1:21; John 6:35; John 11:25; John 14:6; 1 Corinthians 1:30; Colossians 2:9, 10; Hebrews 12:2; 1 John 2:1; Revelation 1:18; Revelation 21:6.
2. Reflect on a time when you experienced the pain of rejection or broken trust.
3. Think of examples from Scripture that demonstrate God's eagerness to restore broken relationships with us.
4. Read Isaiah 53 and make a list of the many things Christ bore in order to redeem us.
5. Reflect on what "leaving the nest" feels like from the perspective of a child, or a parent.
6. Unpack the meaning of the word "atonement."
7. What are some ways you can respond to God's invitation to friendship?

CHAPTER 2

It's Who You Know

*I*n his book *The Little Prince* Antoine de Saint-Exupery describes a conversation between a fox and a small boy. The boy, who asks how he should try to communicate with the fox, is told to say nothing at first. "Words are the source of misunderstanding," says the fox.

Have you ever noticed how misleading the English language can be? If you always took it literally, many common expressions would make no sense at all. For example, ask to buy a yard or a garage at a yard or garage sale, and see what they say. Have you ever seen a body of water? Does that describe someone who just goes with the flow?

Many signs, like "Watch Your Head," seem to ask the impossible. (You're likely to get a whiplash trying that one!) Ever seen "Slow Children Playing"? Do they grow up to be "Slow Men Working"? How about a sign saying, "Clean Restrooms"? You'd think they'd have employees to take care of that!

What about instructions not specific enough, such as "Shake Well Before Using"? Are they referring to you or the can?

Many people have a fear of flying—why do airlines refer to "departing passengers" and call the destination "terminal"?

Some words used together seem mutually exclusive, such as "good grief."

Unfortunately, it can be just as confusing in the religious world. Have you ever wondered about "those on beds of sickness"? If they would just stay off of those beds, they'd probably feel fine. Have you ever been asked to "kneel as far as possible"?

Just how far is it possible to kneel, anyway?

Has a song leader ever asked you to "turn over in your hymnal"? Impossible until they make larger hymnals. It's even harder when a pastor invites you to "turn with me in your Bible."

Perhaps you've been told how important it is to "give God your heart" and wondered how you could do it. Of course it can't be taken literally, but when you try to apply the concept any other way, you find it's no easier. Some say, "You give God your heart by surrendering your will." How do you do that? By "giving your all" or "putting your hand in God's hand"?

Maybe you've been told that no one ever comes to God who does not first "fall on the rock and be broken," but where is the rock and how do you break? Some say you need to use "the eye of faith" and "behold the Lamb." What does that mean?

It gets worse, because Jesus said you need to be "born again." Since you had no control over your first birth, it's easy to wonder what you can do about a second one.

If you feel confused, you're not alone. Nicodemus, one of the brightest religious leaders of Christ's day, had trouble understanding. When Jesus told him about the need for a new birth, Nick responded, "But how can a man be born when he is old? Can he enter a second time into his mother's womb and be born?" (John 3:4, RSV). There ought to be a plain and simple answer to a question this important. There is!

What's the Key?

A group of us were once given a job that required us to unlock a particular door. We had been given a master ring of keys, with the assurance that the key we needed was on that ring. The fellow who had been given the ring tried unsuccessfully to open the door with each of the 30 or so keys that were on it. Some of them would fit the keyhole but would not turn the lock, while others wouldn't even go into the hole. He tried a second time, again without success. A second and third person also tried, but to no avail. I personally tried each key three times without success.

Then the first individual took the door's hinge pins out, only to discover that the position of the door in the jamb would not permit it to come past a certain point. We were frustrated and about to give up when I remembered being told once that some locks in this particular facility required that the key be fully inserted and then pulled out slightly before they would respond. I tried that process with each key on the ring and finally experienced the joy of a familiar turn as the door opened.

I suspect most of the phrases, clichés, and "pat answers" could shed light on how to become or remain a Christian if one knew the correct twist to apply. Not knowing can be an extremely frustrating experience! Not knowing could lead one to the point of giving up in discouragement.

He *Really* Wanted to Know

I can remember, as a 3- or 4-year-old, seeing my preacher father lying on the living room floor of our home. Frequently, pain caused by a bleeding ulcer would place him flat on his back. It wasn't until years later that I came to understand why he had the ulcer.

As he tells it, he was a third-generation Adventist and second-generation pastor. Each Sabbath found him preaching sermons that he recycled from Vandeman, Richards, Fagal, etc. In one of his first churches a saintly little woman would come out after each service to shake his hand. Very kindly, in Christian love she would say, "Pastor, that was a good sermon, but it will be even better when you *know* Jesus."

Dad said he didn't know whether to hit her or hug her. She knew something that other people weren't talking about or perhaps didn't know. She understood that even though Dad knew all the terms, phrases, theology, and doctrines, he didn't *know* Jesus for himself.

It is possible to know the truth and yet not know the One who said, "I am the truth." As a pastor, Dad was experiencing this, and the ulcers began to bleed. He became so frustrated and discouraged that he considered giving up the ministry. And not just the ministry, but faith, Christianity, everything, lock, stock, and barrel.

About that time he was required to attend professional growth meetings for pastors in his locality. While there, under the pretext of "asking for a parishioner," he tried seeking help from his peers. As he dialogued with different pastors, the answers he got seemed vague and unclear:

"What do you tell a parishioner who comes to you and asks, 'How can I really be a Christian?'"

"I tell them that they need to give their heart to God."

"How do you do that?"

"You give your heart to God by beholding the Lamb."

"How do you behold the Lamb?"

"Well, you've just got to surrender your will to His will."

"How do you surrender your will to His will?"

"You have to be born again."

"How can you be born again?"

"You must give Him your all."

"How do you give Him your all?"

"You've just got to put your hand in His hand and walk with Him."

"What if they say 'I can't see Him'?"

"Tell them that they need to use the eye of faith."

"Where do you get the eye of faith?"

"It is given to those who fall on the Rock and are broken."

Needless to say, he left that meeting more discouraged than when he had arrived. He was ready to give it all up, when something seemed to say, "Perhaps you would find help in a book entitled *Steps to Christ*." He got out the book and began reading—underlining everything that it told him to *do*.

When he finished reading *Steps to Christ*, he knew where all those intangible phrases had come from. They were all there: behold the Lamb, the eye of faith, surrender your will, fall on the rock, etc., and he said to himself, "That was sure a lot of help!"

In desperation he decided to read it one more time, this time underlining in red the things it said to do that he *knew how to do*. I'll tell you in a few pages what he found out the second time through the book, but before I do, would you permit a little digression? (I'm trusting you not to skip ahead.)

What *Is* a Christian?

I once took a group of high school students to a Colorado mall to conduct a survey. They were to ask the question "What is a Christian?" and record the responses. Since then, I have asked the same question of church members and students attending church schools. Almost without exception, the answers look like these:

A Christian is somebody who goes to church.

A Christian is somebody who's honest.

A Christian gives faithful tithes and offering.

A Christian doesn't lose their temper.

A Christian is a loyal spouse.

A Christian is a patient father or mother.

A Christian doesn't cheat.

A Christian doesn't lie.

A Christian is kind and loving.

A Christian is concerned about others.

A Christian is helpful.

A Christian cares for the sick.

A Christian feeds the hungry.

A Christian helps the poor.

A Christian is . . .

Do you see the common thread? Every definition has to do with behavior—the way you act, what you do or don't do. Where did they learn these definitions? Could there be a serious misunderstanding here?

If we define Christians as people who are good or nice, we have a problem because some of the nicest folks I have met weren't Christians. In fact, one of the kindest neighbors I ever had was an atheist. It gets even trickier when we consider some of the unpleasant people we've met who call themselves Christians. Mark Twain once said, "When I reflect upon the number of disagreeable people I know who have 'gone to a better world,' I am moved to lead a different life." (He wasn't sure he wanted to go to the "better" world.)

A rich young ruler once asked Jesus, "What must I *do* that I might have eternal life?" (see Matthew 19:16). Many people came to Jesus after He fed the five thousand and asked, "What must we *do* that we might work the works of God?" (see John 6:28). After the Mount Sinai experience the Israelites said, "All that the Lord has said, we will *do*" (see Exodus 24:3). When I ask people what I need to *do* in order to go to heaven, I'm usually given an answer that has to do with trying hard to be good or doing what is right.

Here's a true-or-false question. *If you make it to heaven someday, it will not be because you were good.* Most people answer, "True."

Next true-or-false question. *If you are lost someday, it will not be for being bad.* Was that harder to answer? If you don't go to heaven for being good, it would follow that you don't go to hell for being bad, right? Would Jesus agree with that?

Let me share something with you from E. F. Hutton on eternal life. (You may remember the E. F. Hutton commercial filmed at a New York City intersection. Two men are walking across a crowded street as one asks the other about a particular investment opportunity. The listener replies, "Well, my broker, E. F. Hutton, says . . ." Instantly everybody within sight of the camera freezes and looks in the direction of these two men as a deep, off-camera voice proclaims, "When E. F. Hutton speaks, people listen.")

In John 17:3 Jesus makes *the* summary statement about eternal life. He is the E. F. Hutton on the subject—the last Word, if you will. When He says something about eternal life, people would do well to listen! Here is what Jesus says: "And this is the way to have eternal life—by knowing you, the only true God, and Jesus Christ, the one you sent to earth!" (TLB).

Did He say, "This is life eternal, that they go to church on a particular day"? Or that they do not receive the mark of the beast, or that they have a proper understanding of the state of the dead, or that they do not smoke or drink?

No! He said eternal life is based entirely upon knowing Him and His Father. That's it. If I don't make it to heaven one day, it will be because I didn't know Jesus. If I do make it to heaven, it will be because I got to know Jesus as my friend.

What Does He Mean *Know?*
In Matthew 7 and Luke 13 Jesus tells a story about groups of

people approaching the judge on the final judgment day. The judge asks what claim they have on eternal life, and they answer: "We have cared for the sick and the poor, we have cared for the orphans, we have cast out demons. In Your name we have done many wonderful works."

The judge (that's Jesus) replies, "Depart from Me, you workers of iniquity" (a strange thing to say to people who cared for the sick and orphans, cast out demons, and fed the hungry). Workers of iniquity? Are you used to thinking of social work as evil? Jesus must have a different definition for iniquity than many of us do, or He wouldn't call *those* activities "works of iniquity."

How would you feel if you came back from feeding the homeless and Jesus met you in the church parking lot with the words "Get out of here, you worker of iniquity"? You'd likely be confused. But He doesn't leave us to wonder what that means. He goes on to explain it very simply.

"Depart from me, you workers of iniquity; *I never knew you.*" Conclusion: *anything (even something good)* is considered a work of iniquity if I don't know Jesus! I don't have to murder to be a worker of iniquity, because anything done apart from a personal relationship with Jesus is a work of iniquity. (Those are His words, not mine.)

Matthew 25 contains Jesus' parable about 10 bridesmaids. In that story five of the girls didn't have oil for their lamps, so they went out at midnight to try to buy some. After they finally found oil, they came to the wedding celebration, which was already in progress. (Based upon Jesus' explanation of this parable, the groom represents Jesus, and the wedding celebration represents heaven, after Christ's second coming.) They knocked on the door and said to the Bridegroom, "Lord, let us in."

To which He replies, "Depart from Me; *I don't know you.*"

Have you ever heard someone say, "In order to get into that club or that organization you have to know the right people"? Or "You have to have friends in high places if you want to get in there"? That is what entrance to heaven is all about—*knowing the right people.* Knowing God the Father and Jesus Christ whom He has sent (see John 17:3). The key word here is *know.* Is there a difference between knowing someone and being acquainted with them?

I am not a Greek scholar, but I have a computer Bible that permits me to see the original Greek or Hebrew that each word is translated from. It also gives me the ability to do lightning-quick cross-references of the entire Bible. If I look up a particular word, I can get its definition, derivatives, and all of the different ways the word may be used.

So I decided to try something with the word "know" in John 17:3. First, I searched for cross-references, looking for other places where the Bible contained similar words or ideas. Something startling jumped out at me. One of the cross-references, Matthew 1:25, said that Joseph "knew her [Mary] not till she had brought forth her firstborn son."

Another, Luke 1:34, quotes Mary as saying to the annunciation angel, "How shall this be [becoming pregnant], seeing I know not a man?"

How strange! Why is Jesus' statement about knowing God cross-linked to Joseph not *knowing* Mary until the child was born? Then I pushed a key on my computer that turns English words into their original Greek form. The word "know" *(ginosko, ghin-oce'-ko)* in John 17:3 is the same Greek word used in Matthew where the writer says, "Joseph did not *know* Mary." It is a word that, along with its Hebrew counterpart *(yada', yaw-dah),* is used in Scripture to describe sexual intimacy between a husband and wife.

Clearly, the word "know" that Jesus used in John 17:3 is not a casual knowledge. It's not a surface acquaintance. It's not merely an "I believe" sort of thing. Jesus is talking about a very special, very personal, very meaningful, very significant relationship. Something more than knowing a memory verse or two. Something more than merely attending church once a week. The truth is, sitting in church once a week doesn't make me a Christian any more than sitting in a garage makes me a car.

Would You Call This a Marriage?

The Scene: Bob, a work supervisor in suit and tie, pauses to ask a question out of curiosity. Mrs. Jones is seated at her office desk with her name, MRS. JONES, prominently displayed at the front of the desk. Mrs. Jones chews gum loudly and seems to be somewhat of an airhead. Their conversation follows, with Bob's lines in italics.

Excuse me, Mrs. Jones? Could I ask you a question?

Of course, Mr. Johnson; you're the supervisor!

How long have you worked for us?

Do you mean how long have I worked for Randall and Associates? Or how long have I worked here in the New York office?

I guess I was wondering how long you have worked here in New York.

Well, Mr. Johnson, it will be eight years on June 21. *(pause)* June 21's easy for me to remember, because it's the day after my wedding anniversary.

Oh, really? How many years have you been married?

Eight.

Eight? But didn't you just say you'll have worked here eight years on June 21?

Yeah.

Does that mean you started working for us the day after you got married?

That's right!

What about your honeymoon? When did you go on that?

Didn't have one. I started working for Randall and Associates the next day.

But didn't you and your husband want to go on a honeymoon after the wedding?

Oh, he had to work too.

Where does he work?

BayWorks, Incorporated.

Doesn't sound familiar. Is that around here?

No, it's an engineering firm in San Francisco.

San Francisco! You mean to tell me that you work in New York and your husband works in San Francisco?

The past eight years.

Do you take turns flying back and forth on the weekend?

Are you kidding? I'm afraid of flying.

Then your husband does all the flying so you can be together?

Oh, no! He hates flying too.

Well, it's too far to drive, isn't it?

You got that right!

You guys must own stock in AT&T. Your phone bills have to be outrageous!

Actually, we've never even talked on the phone.

In eight years? Do you write?

Nope.

If you don't mind my asking, when was the last time you guys saw each other?

June 20.

You mean this year, on your anniversary?

No, I mean at our wedding eight years ago.

Let me get this straight: You and your husband haven't seen each other since your wedding eight years ago and you don't write or talk on the phone?

That's right! Hey, you gotta problem with that?

No . . . YOU gotta problem with that! Mrs. Jones—and I almost hesitate to say "Mrs."—I would say you aren't really married.

How can you say that, Mr. Johnson? Joe and I stood up in front of a churchful of people and said our vows. A minister pronounced us husband and wife, and I have a marriage certificate to prove it.

Mrs. Jones, a marriage certificate doesn't make you married any more than a baptismal certificate makes you a Christian.

Really? *(pause)* I must have missed something.

Something More Than "I Do"

Responding to a pastor's altar call is a wonderful start to the Christian life, but if that is where it stops, it hardly qualifies as a deep, personal, intimate relationship. Right?

Taking time to know Jesus in more than a casual way is not only *important* for a Christian; it's imperative. It's not something you do if you have the time. To apply a few common metaphors, it's where the rubber meets the road, it's the least common denominator, ground zero, the bottom line!

Imagine a man who builds a bank. He puts in vaults, computers, and drive-through windows. He hires tellers, then puzzles over his bank's poor success. One day someone asks him, "Have you ever heard of *money?*" He replies *"Money? Could I have missed something?"*

Imagine a baker without flour or a skydiver without a parachute! Those elements are not optional. And knowing Jesus, developing a meaningful relationship with Him, is not optional for the Christian either. It is the basis of the whole business. That's why the apostle Paul says, "What is more, I consider everything a loss compared to the surpassing greatness of knowing Christ Jesus my Lord, for whose sake I have lost all things. I consider them rubbish, that I may gain Christ and be found in him, not having a righteousness of my own that comes from the law, but that which is through faith in Christ— the righteousness that comes from God and is by faith. I want to *know* Christ" (Philippians 3:8-10, NIV).

The most important thing you'll ever occupy yourself with is *knowing* Jesus, becoming better acquainted with Him, learning to love and appreciate Him. When Jesus returns, He's coming back for His *friends,* and I want to be one of them!

A friend is somebody you spend time with. A friend is somebody you talk to. A friend is somebody you enjoy listening to. A friend is somebody you like to do things for. A friend is somebody you have come to know and love.

So how do you get to know an invisible friend? Earlier I told you I'd come back to the rest of the story about my dad's search. Here's where it fits in.

The second time he read *Steps to Christ* (underlining in red what he *knew how to do*) three things stood out:

1. Bible study for the purpose of becoming acquainted with Jesus.
2. Prayer for the purpose of communion with Jesus.
3. Sharing with someone else what you're experiencing in the first two.

These were three things that he knew how to do. He *could* study his Bible to get better acquainted with Jesus. He *could* pray for the purpose of communion instead of simply presenting God with a list of requests. He *could* tell someone else what he found in the first two. These were things he could understand and do. They weren't vague or ambiguous. They were tangible!

In this chapter we have endeavored to show that a meaningful relationship with Jesus is the essence of being a Christian. The chapters that follow will focus specifically on how to develop a personal friendship with Jesus. I want you to *know* Jesus in a practical, tangible way. I want your experience to be the same as that of an old preacher I once read about.

Saying the Psalm

A great actor had just finished giving a live performance, and stood receiving the standing ovation given him by a full house. The applause continued at great length, moving the actor to offer a gesture of gratitude for the audience's kind affection.

"Friends," he said, "as a way of letting you know how much I appreciate you, I would like to take selections from the audience and perform highlights from some of the works I have performed."

Immediately there was a request for a portion of one of Shakespeare's sonnets, which the actor recited with passion and power. Then followed numerous other requests that he performed with rich expression—to the audience's tremendous delight. Finally someone said, "How about the twenty-third psalm? We'd love to hear you say the twenty-third psalm!"

The great actor paused for a moment, uncertain as to whether he remembered the passage. Finally he began, giving it all the color, shape, and expression that he could muster. His voice was majestic as he spoke of the Lord as "my Shepherd"; it softened "beside the still waters"; and almost broke into music with the "restored soul." As he ended "dwelling in the house of the Lord forever," the people rose to their feet again with applause and shouts of "Bravo! Bravo!"

As they were applauding, the great actor noticed someone in the audience he hadn't seen for many years. It was the pastor of the church he had attended as a boy! A rush of memories flooded in as he recalled the way that man had made the stories and teachings of Jesus come alive.

Impulsively he asked the audience if they would permit him to invite the old gentleman to the stage. As the aged man shuffled to the front, the actor told of how Jesus had been made real for them in that congregation so many years ago. Turning to the pastor, he asked him if he would recite the twenty-third psalm again—for them all to hear.

With a different sort of power, the old man began to repeat quietly the words of Scripture—the way an elderly mother might recount some favorite story about her child. When he was done, every eye was overflowing. All, including the great actor, were in tears.

After finally regaining control of his emotions, the actor said, "Friends, I *recited* the twenty-third psalm, and you applauded. My beloved pastor *prayed* the twenty-third psalm, and you wept. I want to tell you why you responded so differently. I knew the twenty-third psalm. But this man *knows the Shepherd.*"

"I consider everything a loss compared to the surpassing greatness of knowing Christ Jesus my Lord. . . . I want to *know* Christ" (Philippians 3:8-10, NIV).

For Further Reflection

Give some additional examples of Christian phrases or concepts that can seem intangible or confusing.

1. Consider Jesus' statement in John 17:3. Why do you suppose definitions for *Christian* so often focus on behavior?
2. Reflect on a situation that was improved because you happened to "know the right person."
3. What are some differences between *knowing* someone and merely being *acquainted* with them?
4. Read Matthew 6:11 and Luke 9:23. What sort of follow-up could one make, after responding to an altar call, that would help nurture a growing experience with Jesus?
5. Reflect on how your relationship with a "best friend" began and grew.
6. What differences might exist between studying the Bible for *information* and studying it to *know* Jesus better?

CHAPTER 3

Born Twice?

*A*nd he spake unto them a parable, saying: Two medical students went off to school to study for medicine. One of the first things they were introduced to was the anatomy lab. In this lab there was a heavy silence. It was kind of cold, and things were really dead there.

But these med students were anxious to make a good showing, so they analyzed the situation. They noticed that there was a good deal of unity there in the lab. There didn't seem to be any fights going on; no one was vying for the highest place. They were all in the same position.

As the med students considered the situation, they became convinced that what these patients needed was improved health. They tried introducing the patients to a new diet, but nobody seemed to care about eating. They told the patients about the benefits of exercise, but no one seemed interested. These students determined there must be an even deeper problem.

They wondered if the problem was a lack of fellowship. But that turned out to be a dead-end street. The patients refused to be sociable. They tried to develop a statement of mission—it was ignored. They considered the lack of resources and took up an offering—no one gave.

In the end, the med students discovered to their dismay that the people in the lab all had a common problem. They were not breathing.

~ ~ ~

I grew up being friends with Kelly. Our parents attended school together, and as the years passed, our families often enjoyed each other's company. My friendship with Kelly continued through elementary school, high school, and college. We did a lot together and enjoyed talking about all kinds of things. We gave each other encouragement and advice, and I remember romances that were improved because I followed Kelly's counsel.

On more than one occasion, friends of mine suggested that I consider dating Kelly. Many of Kelly's friends suggested that she and I would make a great couple. At first neither of us gave the matter much serious thought. Then our parents began dropping hints in that direction, and I remember taking a new look at Kelly.

She was cute, bright, fun to be around, athletic, outdoorsy, and spiritual—all qualities I deemed necessary for a life companion. I'm not sure how many of those adjectives Kelly felt applied to me, but we both decided to seriously pursue a romance together.

Then came an insurmountable problem. Neither of us seemed able to fall in love with the other. We tried! We went on official dates. We worked at it. We agreed that we were *right* for each other. We couldn't imagine having more in common with anyone else. We discussed our inability to "click." Try as we might, there was no red-hot flame; in fact, there wasn't even a spark. It was really quite discouraging to have finally found that *perfect person* and then realize that you would rather swallow gravel than kiss, snuggle, or hold hands. We finally gave up trying.

A few years later I met Marji. The chemistry was there from the start. We didn't try to make it happen; it just did. It was more than a spark, too. It was a nuclear reaction, and less than a year later we were married. We have been kissing, snuggling, and holding hands ever since.

The difference between those relationships was a "click" that transformed the second one into love. Breathless cadavers and self-willed romances have something in common with a message Jesus gave to Nicodemus. They were talking one night about conversion, a "second birth" that Jesus said was necessary before anyone could see the heavenly kingdom. Nicodemus asked Jesus, "How can a person be born again?" *That's a good question.*

The subject of conversion is critical, but it is also problematic, because you can't convert yourself. Conversion is a miracle. So if someone tells you that you need to be converted and you're not converted, what are *you* going to do about it? Can *you* raise the dead?

Can you make yourself fall in love with Jesus by an act of your will? Can you simply say, "I am going to fall in love with Jesus—I am going to appreciate Him and be filled with warm thoughts and earnest devotion"? Is there anything you can do? Did Jesus give any clues to Nicodemus?

Nicodemus

Before we look at what Jesus told Nicodemus, let's first look at Nicodemus. What kind of guy was he? For starters, you're not a member of the Sanhedrin if you're not highly educated. Nicodemus was a "can do" guy. He was what we might call a fourth-generation church member.

The first time Jesus cleansed the Temple, Nicodemus had been standing behind a pillar watching. He saw what happened after the merchants had been sent out—the crowds came in for healing and comfort. Since that time he had been searching the Scriptures trying to find out more about the predicted work of the Messiah. He had begun feeling convicted that Jesus was special and that there was some link between Him and the prophecies that he was reading in the Old Testament.

He inquired to find out where Jesus stayed at night, and finally, under the cover of darkness, he met Jesus. He began by offering compliments: "Rabbi, we know You're a teacher come from God." He was trying to pave the way for a religious discussion. "Could we discuss? Could we talk about religion?"

Is it possible for me to fool myself into thinking I'm a Christian because I can talk for a long time about a scriptural theme? I am not saying that religious studies are not important, but just studying religious material doesn't make me a Christian.

So Nicodemus, this highly educated religious leader who believes that Jesus is special, asks to have a discussion. Jesus looks at him with penetration, and says something that must have startled Nicodemus. He says, "I'm going to tell you the truth, unless a man is born again, he cannot see the kingdom of heaven" (see John 3:3).

For years I assumed that what Jesus meant was "unless you have a conversion experience you can't go to heaven." Careful reading indicates something different from that interpretation.

Nicodemus asks if they can talk about spiritual things, and Jesus instantly replies, "Nicodemus, until you have a rebirth or conversion experience, you can't even *see* spiritual things. They don't even register in your mind. We can't talk about them, because you aren't going to grasp them. You don't have a clue. Spiritual things are spiritually discerned, and spiritual discernment happens only to people who have converted hearts."

Can You See This?

Inside Seattle's Pacific Science Center is a display that tests for color blindness. It consists of 30 individual squares of multicolored shapes and patterns—each with a number camouflaged in its center. People with normal vision can easily see each number. However, a color-blind person cannot see some of the numbers—no matter how hard they try.

As I looked at the display, I realized that I could not see a number in square 11. The interpretation told me that if I didn't see a number in that square, it was because I was color-blind to red. I've always assumed that I can see red, so I asked my daughter if she saw a number in square 11. "Sure," she said. "I see a 13."

A few minutes later my son came along. I called him over. "What do you see in this square?" I asked, pointing.

"I see a 13," he said.

I asked him to show me where in the square it was, so he walked over and traced a 13 with his finger. "It's right here, Dad," he said. But even as he traced, I saw no number.

Suddenly I recalled numerous times, when traveling in the mountains, that I had failed to see flowers my family saw beside the road. When I looked quickly in the direction they pointed, I would often see the lupines and Shasta daisies, but I seldom saw the Indian paintbrush they claimed were there too. Not unless I got out of the car and looked closer could I see those red flowers. I realized then that I can see red, but not when it's embedded in or surrounded by other colors. For 36 years I had not realized I had that problem.

I knew *what* I should be seeing. I had *read* what to look for. People that I knew, loved, and trusted told me *they saw* it. They tried to help me see it. They testified that it was there. They traced the numbers with their fingers, but I still couldn't see. Something would have to happen to my eyes—a miracle of restoration would have to take place in order for me to see the numbers.

That describes exactly the problem we have with unconverted hearts. It's not our fault that we can't see a 13 in square 11. So don't beat yourself up if you can't see. Like the blind men who asked Jesus to open their eyes (see Matthew 20:30-34), you were born unable to see. Seeing is a miracle from heaven.

So Jesus says, "Nick, you can't even *see* the kingdom of heaven until you're born again." Nick had come to talk theology, to talk about religious things, but Jesus was telling him something we all need to understand. Jesus was saying, "It is not theoretical knowledge you need as much as spiritual regeneration. You don't need to have your curiosity satisfied; you need to have a new heart. You must receive new life from above before you can appreciate heavenly things. Until this change takes place, making all things new, it will result in no saving good for us to discuss My story or mission."

A Hard Pill to Swallow?

Did you catch how important conversion is? Don't forget whom Jesus is talking to! A highly educated, denominationally employed, fourth-generation church member. Nicodemus had heard John the Baptist preach, but he'd felt no conviction. He was a "good liver"— he wouldn't think of doing anything wrong. He had a high moral standard. He was benevolent. He was noted for his generosity. He paid a faithful tithe and was liberal in supporting the church with his dollars as well as his energy. He felt secure, and he was startled that there could be a kingdom too pure for him to enter or see.

Nicodemus was struggling. He did not want to think that he could be missing something. He was doing all he knew in order to have it right. To be told that something was missing just didn't feel good.

Jesus had said, "Unless a man be born again, he can't even see the kingdom of heaven." So Nicodemus asks the question that I hope you ask: "How can a man be born when he is old?" (John 3:4, NIV). "How can it happen?" He couldn't seem to understand. *We* can't understand. *We* can't see the number in the square.

In answer to Nicodemus's question, Jesus says, "I'm going to tell you the truth. Unless a man is born of water, and of the Spirit, he cannot enter the kingdom of heaven" (see verse 5).

What's Jesus saying now? He's saying, "Nicodemus, you want to be born again? Well, I'll tell you something. *You* don't have any control over that. It's a Spirit thing. It's supernatural."

Jesus didn't theologize, He didn't debate, but *He did talk about the Spirit.* "Nicodemus, you know how the wind blows? Look, the trees are rustling right now. When the wind blows, you can't see the wind, but you can see the effects of the wind. That's the way it is with the Spirit. You can't see the Spirit, but when He does His work on your heart, you will then be able to see the effect. You will *understand*. There will be a difference. It will be *your* experience, but the *Spirit* will be the one causing it. You could say that it's the Spirit that gives birth" (see verses 6-8).

Is it all clear to you now? Would *you* be feeling better if you'd been Nicodemus? I can almost hear him saying, "Well, OK then! That takes care of everything. Thank you for all these fine answers! I came here to talk about spiritual things, and You tell me I can't see them unless I am born again. I ask how that can happen, and You tell me it's something supernatural that I have no control over. Let's get practical! If I can't make it happen, is there anything I *can do* that would place myself in a more likely or receptive position for the Spirit to do whatever it is You say *He* has to do? There must be something I can do" (see John 3:9).

Remember the Snake?

Here comes Jesus' benchmark statement on the subject of conversion. Here is His answer to Nicodemus's question about whether there is anything *we* can do to avail ourselves of the Spirit's work. In John 3:14, 15 Jesus refers Nicodemus to a story found in Numbers 21:7-9 about a bronze serpent that effected a cure.

Do you recall reading about those people dying from snakebites? Moses was instructed to put a serpent on a pole, remember? What happened after that? If you read it again, you'll discover that anybody who looked in the direction of the uplifted serpent was healed—immediately, miraculously, supernaturally.

Suppose you were bitten by a rattlesnake, and you went to the hospital. Now suppose the emergency room doctor opened up an encyclopedia to a page containing a picture of a rattlesnake, and said, "Here, if you will just look at this picture for a few minutes, you'll be fine."

I bet you'd say, "What kind of doctor or hospital is this? I'm dying of snakebite, and he tells me to look at a snake?"

What was happening in Numbers 21? Something supernatural! It didn't matter if you had been playing with snakes when you got bit—if you looked, you lived. It didn't matter if you had been bitten once before and were healed, then got bitten again and came back to the bronze serpent. No, if you looked again, you were healed again—regardless of how many times you'd been bitten. It didn't matter if you deliberately chose to be bitten, or if you had been playing with the snakes when you were bitten, or if your being bitten was simply an accident. If you looked at the bronze snake you were *healed*. There was life in a look. It happened miraculously. It was supernatural. And the miracle happened only to people who looked. If you didn't look, you died.

Nicodemus asked if there was anything he *could do,* and Jesus says, "Yes! You look in the direction of the uplifted Savior. You focus your eyes on Him, and the Spirit will do what else needs to happen. You want to do something? Look My way. 'I, when I am lifted up from the earth, will draw all people to myself'" (John 12:32, NRSV).

The soul is not enlightened by "proof texts," discussion, debate, or argument. We must look at Jesus to live. Nicodemus received this lesson and carried it with him. He began searching the Scriptures in a new way; not for the discussion of a theory, but in order to receive life for his soul.

Jesus is saying, "If you look My direction [lift Me up], the Spirit's work happens in your heart and you will experience the new birth." You don't have to wait for a preacher to lift Jesus up. You can do that yourself, on a daily basis.

John the Baptist said, "Behold the lamb of God" (John 1:29). Pilate said, "Behold the man" (John 19:5). I wonder if either of them realized they were summarizing the "how to" of the gospel in a sentence. *Look!* There's life in a look. Look at the uplifted Savior. Look at the crucified Savior. Look at Jesus.

I'd like to suggest that you read the Gospel of John. Don't focus on how many people were fed, or how many miracles there were, or which miracle preceded which miracle. Don't read for *information;* read for your soul. Say a prayer before you begin reading, something like this: "Lord Jesus, what I really want is a new heart. What I really want this morning is a new birth, and I can't make it happen. I cannot soften and subdue my heart, but I understand that if I look Your way there is something that the Spirit will do for me that I can't do for myself. So I'm going to look, and I'm asking You to make it worthwhile. I'm asking You to make the miracle take place. I'm asking You to enable me to see the number 13 in square 11. Please make Yourself real for me today."

Pray that prayer and look His way, and don't just do it once or twice. Keep looking, day after day after day, every morning. If Paul is right, that we die daily (see 1 Corinthians 15:31), then the new birth (conversion) would have to be a daily experience as well.

Long or Short Route?

No one ever comes to Jesus who doesn't first feel a need for something better. Nobody. There are two ways to feel a need for Jesus. The best way to gain a sense of need is to look at Him. Lift Him up by reading about Him, meditating on Him, and talking to Him in prayer. As you bow at the foot of the cross and look at Jesus, you will see yourself as sinful and needy, but you will also see Him as *Savior.* That is the shortest route.

But there's another way. It's the way the majority of us do it, and it's the long route home. George McDonald (an author that C. S. Lewis credits with being instrumental in his conversion) describes it this way:

God loves you, and longs for companionship with you. He loves you so much that He will try to woo you to Himself with blessings untold, gift upon gift, favor upon favor. If you fail to respond to His wooing, He loves you so much that He will send out the big dogs of heaven to nip your heels and chase you His direction.

You can wait for the big dogs. You can wait for trouble, failure, heartache, disappointment, and brokenness. You can wait until your world has collapsed and you're lying flat on your back with nowhere to look but up (His direction).

Or you could choose, like Nicodemus did, to look *now* at the uplifted Savior with the purpose of becoming better acquainted with Him as your friend. "Look unto me," He says, "and be ye saved" (Isaiah 45:22).

For Me It Happened Like This . . .

As a senior in high school I was a fourth-generation Christian who knew the answers, knew the doctrines, knew my church's fundamental beliefs, had attended church schools all my life but didn't know Jesus for myself. I was a preacher's kid who pretty much stayed out of trouble, but other than church, I had no personal, private time for God. I knew *about* the truth, but I didn't know the One who *is* the truth. In fact, I didn't even realize that I could or should know Jesus as a personal friend.

One Friday evening I stopped by a friend's house looking for something to do. He invited me to join him and another friend in attending a small Bible study group. These friends were the sort who enjoyed experimenting with drugs for nonmedicinal reasons, and I was incredulous.

I said, *"You and Randy* are going to a Bible study group?"

"Yeah," he said a little hesitantly, "both of us."

A group of about 12 kids from our high school had decided that they wanted to find God. They'd gone to one of our teachers and said, "A group of us would like to get to know Jesus, and we wondered if you'd let us come to your house on Friday nights to read about Him."

He said he would be delighted to share his home for such an activity. So every Friday night he turned his living room over to this group and with his family retreated to the back rooms of the house.

The group had been meeting for some time with a very simple agenda. They read about the life of Christ in the Gospels, they talked with each other about what Jesus meant to them and what they meant to Jesus, and they prayed. That's all they did. Just those three things. And now I was being invited to attend.

"Isn't there something better we could do on Friday night?" I asked.

"Why don't you just give it a try?" Chris said.

I was unaware that during their study this group had stumbled onto the concept of intercessory prayer (praying for others). They had begun an experiment by praying for one guy and one girl from school who seemed seriously uninterested in spiritual things. They wanted to find out if praying for others had any effect, and they had chosen some "hard cases" so they'd be sure to know if it started working. I don't remember who the girl was, but I do know the name of the guy. They prayed for me, without even asking if I minded.

That Friday night I reluctantly decided to go. But I determined that I would go as the devil's advocate. My plan was to raise some unanswerable religious questions and then watch them bend their brains out of shape trying to give answers. I had one in particular, regarding "free choice" and God's foreknowledge, that I was certain would send them for a loop.

Imagine my surprise when I discovered that this group hadn't come to discuss religion (remember Nicodemus?). They were there to talk about Jesus: what He meant to them and what they were discovering that *they* meant to Him. It's very, very difficult to talk about "religious stuff" when everyone is wanting to focus on Jesus. I ended up sitting there speechless as these kids shared from their hearts what Jesus was doing in their lives and why they loved Him.

When people tell you what Jesus means to them, you can't argue with it. You can't get into a debate the way you can when discussing doctrine and "proof texts." You can say you don't believe what they are saying, but they don't care, because like Paul, they "know whom [they] have believed, and are convinced that he is able to guard what [they] have entrusted to him" (2 Timothy 1:12, NIV). They're beaming with the joy of knowing Jesus, and your disbelief doesn't rob them of a thing!

For an hour and a half I watched and listened. Finally they said, "We're going to have prayer now. We're going to kneel and pray conversationally. No one really says 'Amen.' We just pray little sentences until it seems clear that we're through. And nobody prays unless they want to." Then they knelt, but I didn't. They bowed their heads and closed their eyes, but I didn't. I kept mine open to see what these people were going to do.

They began to talk to Jesus. They didn't say, "Please bless the missionaries and leaders of our country." They talked to Jesus like a person talks to their best friend. I felt as though I was eavesdropping on a bunch of private, personal conversations. That living room seemed like it could have been the throne room of heaven.

Without my knowing it, they were also praying inaudibly. You see, when I walked through the door to join their group that night, they were blown away. Nobody said anything to me about it, of course, but I was one of their "prayer experiments," and I had *come.* They gave each other discreet signs, and determined that they were not going to quit praying for me *that night.* And so, silent prayers were ascending all evening, that the Spirit would heal a snakebitten guy as he looked in the direction of the uplifted serpent.

Breakthrough

It happened! When my closest friends started praying and talking to Jesus as you'd talk to a friend, I found myself weeping. I couldn't understand it. I had not come there to weep, yet suddenly I was overcome with tears. I hung my head so they wouldn't see me crying. Prayer finally ended, and everybody left except my two friends. They came over and talked to me about what was happening. They talked about the second birth and how all things become new. They told me about Jesus wanting to be my *friend,* and it clicked. Suddenly I understood for the first time that *Christianity is not about what you do, but about who you know!* And I went home a new creation.

I got home after midnight, woke up early the next morning, and read the entire book of Romans. *This is amazing,* I thought. *This stuff about faith and trust and getting to know a Friend is all right here.* I had never read the Bible through converted eyes before.

As my dad walked by my open door and saw me reading my Bible, he did a double take. Quickly turning around, he ran down the hallway and told my mother, "Lee is reading his Bible!" She couldn't believe it either and had to walk by to see for herself.

When I came out of my room, they were eating breakfast. As I sat down to join them I could hardly contain my enthusiasm for the wonderful "new light" I wanted to share. Excitedly I said, "Dad, did you know—Christianity is not about what you *do.* It's about who you *know.* In fact, Jesus is more interested in becoming our friend than in He is in our performance, because He knows that if we can become friends, *that* will change us! Isn't that cool?"

I love my preacher father for his response that morning. He didn't say to me, "You idiot! That's been the only string on my violin for the past 20 years. Where has your head been when you are in church?" No, he didn't say that. All he said was "Isn't that *wonderful?*"

Then I went to church and stayed for both services. Can you imagine my surprise on the front row when Dad began to preach about the very stuff I'd told him at breakfast? I couldn't believe he'd managed to work that into his sermon on such short notice!

What had happened? Had my father changed his sermon for me? No, I suddenly could see the number 13 in square 11. A miracle had happened. How had it happened? I had put myself in a place where the Son was lifted up, and the Holy Spirit drew me to Jesus.

I am glad that Jesus wants to do for us exceedingly, abundantly, above all that we could ask or think (see Ephesians 3:20). I'm thankful that He has promised to do for us what we cannot do for ourselves. May He help us to recognize our great need and save us from having to wait until the "big dogs" are let loose. May His Spirit create in us new hearts, enabling us to see Jesus more clearly and love Him more dearly.

Lift Him up every day. Be born again. There is life in a look— at Jesus.

For Further Reflection

1. Reflect on the differences between approaching a task you have a passion for and one you have simply been assigned to complete.
2. After reading Matthew 23:1-35, describe four of Jesus' main concerns regarding Pharisees. Are you aware of anything pharisaical in yourself?
3. After reading Matthew 13:13-15 and 2 Corinthians 4:3, 4, describe the difficulty facing the unconverted when it comes to spiritual things.
4. According to John 1:12, 13, John 3:5-8, and Titus 3:5, who is responsible for conversion or the new birth?
5. In your own words, summarize Isaiah 45:22 and John 12:32.
6. Read Numbers 21:4-9 and make a list of the conditions to be met in order for healing to take place. (This might be a trick question.)
7. As practically as possible, apply the lesson in the illustration of the bronze serpent toward the experience of conversion.
8. Is conversion, or the new birth, necessary more than once? See 1 Corinthians 15:31.

CHAPTER 4

Time Well Spent!

*W*e have tried to show from Scripture that *knowing Jesus* is what Christianity is all about. We have pointed out the privilege and need of a personal relationship with Christ. But how do you get acquainted with Somebody you can't see? How do you have a daily devotional life, or quiet time with Jesus, that is meaningful and real? I'd like to offer you a "spiritual prescription" for developing a friendship that will last forever. I inherited it from my dad, and it goes like this:

> TIME ALONE AT THE BEGINNING OF EVERY
> DAY, IN CONTEMPLATION OF THE LIFE OF
> JESUS THROUGH HIS WORD AND THROUGH
> PRAYER.

Pray First

Let's break the prescription down and take a closer look at the various components. In the film *The Sound of Music,* Maria gives a lesson in music fundamentals by singing a song that begins:

> Let's start at the very beginning,
> A very good place to start!
> When you read you begin with A-B-C,
> When you sing you begin with do-re-mi.

When you spend time alone with Jesus for the purpose of knowing Him as your friend, *begin* with prayer. Every morning as I begin my own quiet time with Jesus I pray for three specific things.

First, I ask that the Holy Spirit will make Jesus *real* for me. I ask that He will increase my sense of appreciation for Jesus, and that I will see Jesus as more than a figure in history. I don't want just to know where He went, what He said, or what He did. I want to know *Him!*

Second, I ask for spiritual eyesight. In John 3 Jesus told Nicodemus that spiritual things are spiritually discerned, and that human beings need something extra from the Holy Spirit in order to grasp the deeper meaning in God's Word. That's why I ask for spiritual eyeglasses and hearing aids.

Third, I ask that Satan and his demons be prevented from distracting me. Satan is a master of distraction and will use anything (good or bad) to lead my thoughts so far off track that I wander halfway around the world without even realizing it. I have experienced a similar thing when trying to study for college exams. It's terrible to read the same paragraph five times and still not know what you've read! So I pray every morning that God will rebuke Satan's power to distract me.

Inspired Reading

Next, begin reading something specifically about Jesus. If you want to do a theological study on the feast days of the Old Testament, that's OK, but I suggest that for your quiet time (for the purpose of knowing Jesus) you pick material clearly *about Jesus.*

Even in the Bible there are places where He is more clearly revealed than others. All of God's Word is inspired, but within that inspired book are two kinds of scripture. I'm going to call them *informational* and *inspirational. Informational* verses include such things as genealogies and detailed instructions for building a tabernacle. *Inspirational* scriptures will leave your heart strangely warmed by the love of God and the matchless charms of Jesus.

Remember, the purpose of the devotional life is to become better acquainted with Jesus. In reading for that purpose, I can do better than 1 Chronicles 1:50, where I'm told that "When Baal-Hanan died, Hadad succeeded him as king. His city was named Pau, and his wife's name was Mehetabel daughter of Matred, the daughter of Me-Zahab" (NIV).

That information is there for a reason. The genealogies and family trees show us that Jesus came by the right family, just as prophecy said He would come. They point to Jesus, but if you're trying to grow closer to Him by reading the names of who begat whom, and how many children they had, it may be a long, hard winter.

Jesus once told a group of church leaders, "You search the Scriptures, for in them you think you have eternal life; and these are they which testify *of Me*" (John 5:39, NKJV). On Resurrection Sunday, "beginning at Moses and all the prophets," He showed two travelers on the road to Emmaus, "in all the scriptures the things concerning himself" (Luke 24:27).

The story is told about a preacher who brought a puzzle home one evening in hopes that it would sidetrack his young children long enough for him to get some rest after a hard day. He'd chosen a puzzle that was a world map, thinking that his children's ignorance of geography would lengthen the time necessary to complete the puzzle. Imagine then his surprise and disappointment when shortly after taking the puzzle into the other room, his children returned to tell him it was finished. As he looked at it in disbelief, he asked how they had managed to put it together so quickly. "Oh, it was easy, Daddy. On the back side of the puzzle is the picture of a man. Once we put the man together, the world was all right."

The whole Bible is a biography about Jesus. There is a Man in it! For those who have become familiar with Jesus in the more obvious places, He can be recognized peeking out from between every line and back of every word. In fact, it is only as we see Jesus in the Scriptures that it really takes on meaning. There is a Man in the Bible, and the devotional life is about looking for the Man!

In order for devotional reading to be most effective, it is best to use a Bible written in an easy-to-read style. The translation or paraphrase that works best will vary with individuals, but many have found the New International Version to be a favorite. Some would suggest avoiding paraphrased versions of the Bible, but devotional reading is for your *heart,* not exegesis! For that reason you'll do best picking a version you enjoy.

Hands or fingers once tender and sensitive will grow hardened or calloused when exposed repeatedly to gardening or carpentry. Similarly, one can become gospel-calloused; cycling through a variety of books on the life of Jesus can help keep His story fresh and alive. For this reason I've become a collector of books and videos on the life of Jesus. There is something attractive and refreshing about reading the old, old story written in a new way or from a unique perspective. See Appendix A for a list of favorites.

Time—How Much?

Our prescription included *time alone at the beginning of every day in contemplation of the life of Christ.* How much time? Perhaps you've heard the story about Martin Luther, who was quoted as saying, "I have so much to do each day that I can't begin to accomplish it all if I don't first spend at least four hours in prayer." Sounds a bit overwhelming, doesn't it?

I remember kneeling for personal prayer at the living room couch about 10:00 p.m. one night, after the rest of my family had gone to bed. Suddenly I was aware of my wife tapping me on the shoulder. Somewhat startled, I asked her what she wanted. She answered by asking me when I was coming to bed.

I told her I would be there in a minute, and was a bit annoyed when she asked me what I was doing. *"Praying!"* I answered rather piously.

She said, "Do you know what time it is?"

"No, what time is it?" I asked.

"It's 2:00 in the morning."

"Well," I answered smugly, "I have a lot to say." (Me and Martin Luther, a couple of birds-of-a-feather prayer-warriors types.)

She decked me with her last question, however. "How come there's a drool spot on the couch where your head was resting?" And I knew I had miles to go before I could keep up with Martin.

Many years ago I watched a talk show host interview Arnold Schwarzenegger, the bodybuilding expert. Arnold, who had won

Mr. Universe several years in a row, was wearing a blue polyester suit and holding a dumbbell in each hand. While doing dumbbell repetitions, he talked about how to develop an exercise program by picking weights suitable to one's level of fitness and strength. He said that over time one would find it natural to increase the amount of weight and the number of repetitions, but he warned not to start with what he or other weight lifters did.

As Arnold was once more emphasizing the importance of picking a routine that works (while lifting the dumbbells as easily as one might lift their arm to swat a fly), the host asked how much weight Arnold was lifting with the dumbbells. Arnold answered, without breathing hard or even breaking a sweat, "100 pounds each, but remember—don't feel that you have to duplicate my routine. The important thing is not how much you lift, but that you begin a routine."

I was into rock climbing at the time, and had been doing a lot of upper-body building for that sport. I thought that because I could do 50 pull-ups without stopping I was in pretty good shape, so I went down to a local gym with the idea of trying out their dumbbells. I knew better than to try 100-pound dumbbells, so I put about 30 pounds on each hand bar and then tried lifting my left arm in the manner Arnold had described. *H'mm,* I thought, *perhaps I should try using my stronger arm.* If someone had been watching, they would probably have wondered how long I was going to stand there before lifting. I set them down and took off a few pounds in an effort to find the weight that was "right for me." I finally discovered that if I removed all weights from the bars, I could lift the bars effortlessly. Arnold had been right when he said that trying to do what others do would lead to discouragement!

As you develop your devotional life, don't seek to copy Martin Luther. That will just lead you to discouragement. The important thing is not how much time you spend, but that you start with something. As you take some daily time to get better acquainted with Jesus, you will find your spiritual appetite increasing. Don't time yourself or watch the clock! Remember, the time you spend with Jesus is not for the purpose of making sure you have done your devotional duty for the day. That's righteousness by relationship, which is a first cousin to righteousness by works. The purpose of daily quiet time with Jesus is to become better acquainted *with Him*.

Experts say that intentional quality time together is an important part of a healthy marriage. Would you watch the clock while spending time with a spouse? Would you want to know the minimum amount of quality time required in order to have a healthy relationship? How would you feel if your spouse said, "Honey, let's get our 15 minutes of quality time in for today"? A relationship like that is not likely to grow by leaps and bounds!

How much time should you spend with Jesus? Don't look for minimums, but spend some time with Him, and let Him increase your appetite. He is big enough to handle that. After all, He promised in Philippians that the work He started in you He would complete.

Time—Doing What?

The Desire of Ages, a classic on the life of Christ, contains this thought: "It would be well for us to spend a thoughtful hour each day in contemplation of the life of Christ. *We should take it point by point, and let the imagination grasp each scene, especially the closing ones.* As we thus dwell upon His great sacrifice for us, our confidence in Him will be more constant, our love will be quickened, and we shall be more deeply imbued with His spirit" (p. 83; italics supplied).

Would you like a deeper sense of appreciation for Jesus? Would you like your confidence in Him to be more constant? Would you like to be more inclined to trust in and depend on Him? If we will spend some time each day contemplating, meditating, and allowing our imagination to dwell on Jesus' life, those things will happen!

As an aid in meditation, many have found it helpful to keep a notepad or journal in which they write down the imaginings that come to mind while contemplating a verse or passage of Scripture. As you read a verse, try to imagine yourself there. What would it have been like to be in the crowd? Picture the little children running to Him, squealing and calling His name.

If you don't hurry past Mark 10:13-16, you just might see Jesus holding His arms open wide as He says over His shoulder to the disciples, "Let the little children come to Me, and don't discourage them from coming" (see verse 14). Then see Him laughingly catch up the first one to reach Him and toss him into the air. Perhaps the child is shirtless and you catch Jesus making spluttering noises as He blows on the little fellow's stomach. Watch Him get down on His knees with the whole gang of kids and dig sand castles on the shores of Galilee.

Can you see that? That's what it means—"Let your imagination grasp each scene." As you do you'll find your appreciation, love, and confidence in Him growing. You'll realize that if He had the time for children, He must have time and attention for *you*.

One-on-One

Time and attention for you *personally!* Jesus is interested in the entire human race, but He is specifically interested in *you*. In order for your friendship with Him to grow, you need to have times you and He are one-on-one. Church is good, family worship is great, and group Bible study can be meaningful, but they are no substitute for one-on-one time with Jesus.

In John 6 Jesus called Himself the Bread of Life and compared Himself to the manna that fed Israel as they journeyed toward Canaan. He repeatedly urged His listeners to eat "the bread which came down from heaven" (verse 41). Most of us eat two to three meals every day in order to be healthy and strong in a physical sense. Jesus chose the bread metaphor to remind us that we need to "eat" *spiritually* on a daily basis as well. No one can eat for another. Sometimes someone will jokingly say, "He ate enough for both of us." But the truth is, I cannot satisfy your hunger by eating extra for you.

In John 4 Jesus compared Himself to water as well (another daily necessity). Suppose you were really thirsty and someone said they were going to get a drink. What if you asked them to kindly bring you a drink also, and they returned saying, "There were no cups, so I just drank a little more for you"? Would your thirst be quenched? Of course not! You have to drink for yourself. Even if they brought a cup of water back, they still couldn't drink it for you.

That is why in Exodus 16:16 the people were instructed to "gather [the manna] every man according to his eating." You must have a *personal* experience with Jesus. It's not enough to depend on mom or dad, husband or wife, teacher or preacher. You must eat for yourself.

If I consistently choose not to eat physical food, it is likely that I have a eating disorder and will die if it is not corrected. Karen Carpenter died from anorexia. Her tragic ending is all the sadder when you realize that she didn't need to die. It would be an even greater tragedy to be a spiritual anorexic! How strange, then, that so many try to subsist spiritually by eating only once a week in church.

Time—When?

I love the way the Bible begins in Genesis 1:1 by saying, "In the beginning God." I may be extrapolating something from Scripture that's not intended, but I think that is great advice for *when* to spend some meaningful time with Jesus. "In the *beginning* God." Begin your day with God.

In Exodus 16:21 we discover that "when the sun grew hot, [the manna] melted" (NIV). Manna melts! It can be a real challenge to slow down and focus on time alone with Jesus if you wait until the day is well under way. The manna came down from heaven to give the people strength for the day. When do you need daily strength? At the beginning of the day, or after it's over? Nutritionists and doctors tell us that a good breakfast is the most important meal of the day. They say that if you are going to eat only one meal a day, the one to eat is breakfast.

"One of the secrets of a meaningful, consistent relationship with God," says Morris Venden, "is to schedule it at sometime earlier than those last few minutes before you go to bed at night, when you can't keep your mind on a subject and you fall asleep praying."

I am not saying it is wrong to fall asleep praying. I used to feel guilty about that until I mentioned it to my father once. He responded by asking, "What's wrong with that?"

I answered, "Well, it seems a lot like hanging up in the middle of a phone conversation, and that's not very polite."

Dad replied, "I call it pillow talk, and I can't think of a better way to fall asleep than while talking to God!"

So it's OK to fall asleep at night while praying, but for building your relationship with Jesus I'd suggest that you set aside time for Him when you can be fresh enough to stay awake and become better acquainted. There really is something about the early-morning hours, after the mind has been at rest and before the distractions or responsibilities of the day have begun clamoring for our attention.

"But," you say, "I'm not a morning person! I *need* my sleep. Talk to me before noon at your own risk. It would be easier for a chicken to grow lips than for me to get up early in the morning."

Not so fast, partner. I've got exciting news for you! If you take a look at Isaiah 50:4, you'll discover that "he wakens me morning by morning, wakens my ear to listen like one being taught" (NIV). I believe that Jesus is so interested in fellowship with you, so interested in growing a friendship with you, so interested in spending quality time with you, that *He* is willing to wake you up for just such an appointment.

Remember, this is the same Person who said in Revelation 3:20, "Look! I am standing at the door, and I am constantly knocking. If anyone hears me calling him and opens the door, I will come in and fellowship with him and he with me" (TLB). He is standing just outside, *asking* for an invitation. I believe Jesus is so interested in spending quality time with you that if you ask Him to wake you for the purpose of getting better acquainted with Him, He will do it!

It doesn't matter whether or not you are a morning person, or whether you think you can't get up before the manna begins melting. If the sincere desire of your heart is that you might have quiet time enough to begin your day with Jesus, ask Him to fulfill the promise of Isaiah 50:4 for you. Then respond by getting up when He *does* wake you—even if it seems like an "ungodly" hour. (You may want to ask Him to give you a kick, rattle, or shake to ensure that you are alert enough for fellowship!)

More than 15 years ago I shared the principle of Isaiah 50:4 with my wife, Marji, who has used Jesus as her wake-up call almost exclusively ever since—and never known Him to fail. It doesn't matter what time she goes to bed or what time she needs to get up in the morning. She has discovered that Jesus sees to it that they have quality time together. And it's worth noting that she's never missed a morning appointment—He always wakes her early enough.

I believe that the tithing principle transfers into the devotional life. I cannot explain to people who don't tithe how it is that 80 or 90 percent of my paycheck (with God's blessing) goes further than 100 percent without it. Nobody understands *that* if they haven't tried it. It is a miracle of divine grace that I can have more buying power with less money, but I have never known it to be otherwise.

Did you know that same principle applies to your night's rest? If you will covenant with Jesus to get up earlier for the purpose of spending time with Him, He will add a special blessing to the time that is left in your day, and you will find that six or seven hours of sleep with God's blessing goes farther than eight or nine hours without it. A divine miracle of grace will give you more energy and strength, and make you more efficient than you would have been with a "full night's rest." There is no such thing as running out of gas because you got up early to spend time with Jesus.

Isaiah 40:29-31 promises, "He gives power to the weak, And to those who have no might He increases strength. Even the youths shall faint and be weary, And the young men shall utterly fall, but those who wait on the Lord shall renew their strength; they shall mount up with wings like eagles, they shall run and not be weary, they shall walk and not faint" (NKJV). And God speaks through Proverbs 8:17 to say, "I love them that love me; and those that seek me early shall find me."

A Worthy Example

According to Scripture, Jesus Himself made time alone with God His first priority. No other life was ever as crowded with labor and responsibility as His; yet how often He was found in prayer! How constant was His communion with God! Again and again in the history of His earthly life are found records such as these: "Rising up a great while before day, he went out, and departed into a solitary place, and there prayed" (Mark 1:35). "Great multitudes came together to hear, and to be healed by him of their infirmities. And he withdrew himself into the wilderness, and prayed" (Luke 5:15, 16). "And it came to pass in those days, that he went out into a mountain to pray, and continued all night in prayer to God" (Luke 6:12).

In 1996 my wife and I had the privilege of actually visiting the ruins of Capernaum. As we stood looking at what is said to be Peter's house, I imagined the Sabbath that Jesus healed Peter's mother-in-law, who had been suffering with a high fever. In my mind's eye, I could picture boisterous, outspoken Peter, clambering up to his rooftop and announcing the miracle to the town.

Conscientious Jews would not travel even short distances on the Sabbath, but I bet the news traveled to every part of town that day! Everybody knew that Jesus was there, and when the Sabbath was past, the whole town began making its way to Peter's house. No one knew whether the morning would come and find the Healer still among them. So they came and lined up at Peter's door, waiting to see Jesus. Those sick and infirmed, blind and deaf, poor and outcast all stood in line for a chance to see the One who never turned a sufferer away.

Checking an astronomical guide, I learned that the sunset (indicating Sabbath's end) did not take place at that time of year until about 9:00 p.m. The town's people had waited till then to come for healing, but even though it was late, the Great Physician didn't rush them through His "clinic." I've gone to see doctors who kept me waiting for hours and then spent three minutes with me before sending me away with a prescription and a bill for $100. But I see Jesus talking with each sufferer, answering questions, being friendly—as though He was the one who invented time. Jesus took time with those people, and we are told that it was far into the night before the last sufferer retired to his home and Jesus lay down to sleep.

As I stood in Capernaum looking at Peter's house, I pictured Jesus finally lying down on the stone floor and pulling a blanket over Himself, well after midnight. And then I thought of Mark's description of the next morning: "Rising up a *great while before day,* he went out and departed into a solitary place, and there prayed" (Mark 1:35). I could just see Him stirring there on the floor, stretching a bit, then quietly getting to His feet, careful not to stir the still-sleeping family. No doubt he folded His blanket in a customary way (remember Resurrection morning?) and then quietly opened the door and headed up the hill just above Peter's place. He was headed for an appointment that He wouldn't dream of missing (or miss by dreaming).

In a life completely devoted to the good of others, Jesus found it necessary to withdraw from the hustle and bustle of travel and from the crowd that surrounded Him day after day. He had to turn aside from a life of ceaseless activity and contact with human needs to seek a quiet place for uninterrupted communion with His Father. Like us, He was completely dependent upon God, and in the secret place of prayer He sought divine strength. Communion with God was where He found comfort and joy. His life is our example. (See *The Desire of Ages,* pp. 362, 363.)

Time—How Often?

There is one more lesson from the manna that we need to include in this chapter. According to Exodus 16:19, no one was to "leave of it till the morning." What happened to the manna if people tried to save yesterday's for another day? The manna rotted. In fact, it bred worms and stank!

Remember, Jesus compares Himself to manna, and the principle worth noting here is that *yesterday's* experience is not good enough for *today.* You need a fresh experience with Jesus every day. Don't depend on the past, or your last visit to church. I always wince when I hear prayers offered in church that include a request that God will provide something in the worship service that "will get us through another week." No! Time with Jesus *every day* is what gets one through the week. As the bumper sticker says: "Seven days without Jesus makes one weak!"

But perhaps you are saying, "Where am I going to find time for one more thing? I'm just too busy already! I don't need more *sleep;* I need more *time.* I'm a single parent . . . I'm a college student . . . I'm the mother of three preschoolers . . . I have to work two jobs just to pay all the bills . . . I'm putting two kids through college . . ."

Amy was a student of mine at the Christian high school where I taught Bible. I had been sharing with my students both the need and the privilege of having a personal relationship with Jesus. One evening Amy gave a worship talk to the student body and staff of our school.

"A while back," she said, "I slept in to the point of being pressed to make it to my first period class on time. A test was scheduled for that morning, so in a hurry, I said, 'Lord, You'll have to understand that I'd like to spend some time with You right now, but I'm in a huge hurry! I'll have to catch up with You later, or I'll be late to class. But please go with me today.'"

With that she jumped up and rushed into the bathroom, where she began brushing her teeth. As she stood in front of the mirror, she began having an imaginary conversation with her reflection. She said it was as if her reflection asked, "What are you doing?"

Annoyed by the fact that it seemed so obvious, she somewhat impatiently answered her reflection by responding, "I'm brushing my teeth!"

The girl in the mirror wasn't easily "brushed" off, and asked, "Well, why are doing that?"

"Because," Amy answered, "I wouldn't dream of going out in public with rotten breath. I could never meet my friends without having brushed my teeth first."

In a flash of insight, the girl in the mirror said, "Oh, I see. You have enough time for the things that are *really* important to you. Apparently having good breath is more important to you than spending time with Jesus."

At that point Amy quit talking to her reflection and said, "Lord, please forgive me. I will take an unexcused tardy to my class if I need to, but I want to start my day by beginning it with You." She sat down with her Bible and went late to class only to discover that the teacher had called in sick and postponed the test.

We have the time for what's important. And if you decide that spending time with Jesus is important, you'll *find* or *make* the time for it. I won't tell you it is going to be easy. It is called the *fight* of faith. But I will tell you that Jesus is worth fighting for!

The Banquet Table (a parable)

"Here I am! I stand at the door and knock. If anyone hears my voice and opens the door, I will come in and eat with him, and he with me" *(Revelation 3:20, NIV).*

When I awoke in the morning, the table was there. Perhaps it had been there before, but I had never noticed it. It was such a large table, so colorfully spread, that I can't imagine how anyone could have missed it.

I approached the table for a closer look and was greeted by a tall Man, apparently the host. "Come and dine," He said joyfully. "Would you like for Me to show you to a seat?"

I hesitated. "Well, I'm not sure. Could I ask You a few questions first?"

"Certainly," He replied.

"Whose banquet is this—I mean, who prepared it? Who is issuing the invitations?"

He said, "The Spirit and the bride say, 'Come!' And let him who hears say, 'Come!' Whoever is thirsty, let him come; and whoever wishes, let him take the free gift of the water [and bread] of life" (Revelation 22:17, NIV).

"You mean I don't have to pay anything?"

"That's right."

"I don't usually get that hungry for breakfast," I said as I considered the offer. I looked hopefully up and down the table. "You don't happen to have some of those breakfast bars that I could just stick in my pocket and eat on my way to work? It would sure save time."

The Host smiled. "If you sit down and eat, you'll find that you have more appetite than you think you do, at least most of the time."

Still I hesitated. "I've known some people who started out eating breakfast, and the next thing it was breakfast, dinner, and supper. Then they added a few snacks in between. Finally, they were eating all day long and got so fat they could hardly walk around."

"It's true," the Host replied, "that those who do nothing but eat will grow fat. But it is equally true that those who don't eat will die."

He was winning me to His side—but then I noticed something. Sitting on the far side of the table was the preacher from my church. His plate was filled with good things, and he was eating with obvious enjoyment.

"Oh, look! There's my preacher!" I said to the Host.

"Yes," He responded. "He's here every morning. He is a great believer in eating a good breakfast."

"That's wonderful!" I said. "That will save me a lot of time, because I go to hear him every week. He can tell me what the food is really like and I won't have to take the time to come here and eat for myself."

"No one can eat for another," the Host responded. "In order for you to receive strength and nourishment, you must come and eat."

Just then I caught sight of another familiar face. There was Billy Graham down at the end of the table. "Does he come here every day too?" I asked the Host.

"Yes, he's here for several hours every morning."

"Several hours?" I gulped. "Then I'd better not come. Because I know I don't have enough of an appetite to eat for that long."

"You're only expected to eat for your own needs, not for someone else's," replied the Host. "This is your first morning. Maybe for today you'll want to start out with a couple of those thin, crispy breadsticks and a glass of juice. You'll be surprised how quickly your appetite will grow as long as you continue to balance your eating with the proper exercise."

I was just about ready to ask Him to show me to a place at the table when I thought of one more thing. "Hey, wait a minute! This whole business suddenly sounds pretty legalistic. You wouldn't want me coming here to Your banquet table just out of habit, would you?"

"I can't think of another 'habit' that would bring you greater health," said my Host. "But you're missing the point. I'm here every day, waiting to serve you, waiting to share good things that I have prepared for you. I'm here, the table is here, there's a place for you here. I really look forward to having your company for breakfast; why would you just walk by the table and go on your way? It's here, it's free, it's for you."

Then He took my hand and led me to my place at the table. He filled my plate with grapes and cherries and strawberries and waffles . . . but wait! I'm telling you about *my* meal. Your favorite things may be entirely different. Why don't you come to the banquet and eat for yourself?

For Further Reflection

1. What is the longest you've ever gone without eating? without drinking?
2. What spiritual application can be made between Jesus' claim in John 4:14; John 6:32-35; John 6:47-51, and your answer to the first question?
3. Make a practical application regarding Jesus' statement about His words in John 6:63. How can you "eat" the "Bread of Life"?
4. Make note of some especially inspiring scriptural passages about Jesus that are found in books other than the four Gospels.
5. Reflect on some of the parallels between how an athlete develops skill and how spiritual growth is to be gained through the reading of God's Word.
6. Reflect on occasions when God has fulfilled the promise of Isaiah 40:29-31 for you.
7. What differences might exist between a snack-bar approach to God's Word and a full-meal approach?

CHAPTER 5

Be Still and Know

$\mathcal{P}$rayer is communion with God—conversing with Him as you would converse with a friend. How do you converse with friends? Do the bulk of your conversations consist of asking for favors? To limit prayer to request is like attending a musical concert where the audience merely reads sheet music.

When I was in college I had a friend named Bill. Anytime Bill called me on the phone, found me in the dorm, or joined me in the cafeteria, I knew what to expect. After he had asked how I was doing, or what I thought of the weather, he would always ask for a favor. It got to be so predictable that once, when he called on the phone, I cut to the chase and said, "Bill, what did you call to *ask* for?"

Startled, he replied, "Well, I was wondering if I could borrow your skis."

Would you consider it a meaningful friendship if all you ever heard from somebody was "Could I please have this?" or "Would you help me with that?" The Bible is more than a Sears catalog, and God is more than a celestial Santa.

The promises in the Bible weren't put there so we could *claim* them. They were written to show us how much the *Promisor* loves us. Too often we get short-circuited and focus on the promises. Some have even counted them. I'm thankful for the promises, but I'm more thankful for the Promisor. If it weren't for Him, there would be no value in the promises.

Why do earthly parents make promises to their children?

Because they love them and enjoy doing things for them. Because they wish to show affection. Because they love being involved with their children. Our heavenly Father is like that too. He has told us about wonderful things He wants to do for us because He loves us and enjoys our company. If we forget that, we've missed the point.

Keep your wants, your joys, your sorrows, your cares, and your fears before God. You cannot burden Him; you cannot weary Him. He who numbered the hairs of your head is not indifferent to the wants of his children. "The Lord is full of compassion and mercy" (James 5:11, NIV). *His heart of love is touched by our sorrows and even by our speaking of them.*

Take to Him everything that perplexes the mind. Nothing is too great for Him to bear (He rules the universe], . . . Nothing that in any way concerns our peace is too small for Him to notice. There is no chapter in our experience too dark for Him to read; there is no perplexity too difficult for Him to unravel. No calamity can befall the least of His children, no anxiety harass the soul, no joy cheer, no sincere prayer escape the lips, of which our heavenly Father is unobservant, or in which He takes no immediate interest. "He heals the brokenhearted, and binds up their wounds" (Psalm 147:3, NKJV).

The relationship between God and each person is as distinct and full as though there were not another soul upon the earth to share His watchcare, or for whom He gave His beloved Son. It is easy to talk about anything with somebody like that!

Paraphrased from *Steps to Christ*, p. 100.

Love to Talk

Why do people in love enjoy associating with each other? Shortly after I met Marji, I began finding every excuse I could to go to the girls' dorm and sit with her in the lobby. We enjoyed being together so much that many times we would just sit and grin at each other—without even saying a word. When we did talk, we'd lose track of time until the dean came to shoo me out for the night. When that happened I'd go back to my room and call Marji on the phone. Why? Because we were in love. We took time for each other because we valued our relationship.

Childlike

Suppose we asked a little boy, "Why do you always run to your mother with your joys and fears?" He'd probably wonder how anyone could ask such a question. Mother solves his problems. Mother is the source of wisdom. Mother understands. Mother kisses away bruises and wipes away tears. And sometimes a little boy runs to his mother just to hear her say, "I love you," or to see her smile, or to get a hug.

Jesus said, "Unless you . . . become like little children, you will never enter the kingdom of heaven" (Matthew 18:3, NIV). A child listens awhile. A child is expectant. A child finds it easy to kneel. A child plays and sings. A child laughs at itself. A child trusts even when it doesn't understand. A child enjoys *talking with someone it loves.*

Christians might wonder how anyone could ask the question "Why pray?" True, Christians ask for daily bread, knowing that their unbelieving neighbors get bread without asking. Christians know that God feeds the ravens, sparrows, *and* the wicked, too. But Christians pray because they receive something *along with* their daily bread. They receive the *companionship* of God. That is far more valuable than daily bread. Jesus said, "Man does not live on bread alone" (Matthew 4:4, NIV).

We often talk about praying for an answer, overlooking the fact that the *answer is prayer!* The privilege of talking with God and knowing that we have His fellowship, communion, and listening ear is the most wonderful thing about prayer.

As a child grows, the father knows that his boy or girl needs more than food and clothes. He knows his child needs companionship, fellowship, counsel, and understanding.

Keith Miller tells how his 4-year-old daughter would come every night and ask him to read her the story of Goldilocks and the three bears. She'd crawl up on his lap and laugh or giggle as he read. Then she'd thank him, and the next night ask him do it all over again.

One day he made a cassette tape of himself reading the story and gave it to her, along with a child's tape player. He told her that every time she wanted to hear the story, she could get the book out and then push the button to listen.

She tried it one night but got only halfway through before bringing the book to Daddy. "I want *you* to read the story to me," she said.

When Keith asked why, she replied, "Because I can't sit on the tape recorder's lap."

What did she mean? What did she need? It wasn't the story; it was the *companionship* that made the difference for that little girl.

Could God know that we need the Father's companionship too? Even if *we* don't know it? He gives food and blessings to everybody. But He wants to give even more. Being a companion is *important to Him too.*

Keith, a teacher friend of mine, had a son who went away to school for his eleventh-grade year. One day I saw Keith after Adam had been away for about a month.

I asked him how it was going with Adam gone. Tears came to his eyes as he answered, "It's *terrible!* I used to drive the school bus, and Adam would ask to ride with me instead of coming later. I'd tell him he could sleep longer if he came in the car, but he'd reply, 'No, Daddy, I want to go with you.'"

"I'd ask him why he wanted to go so *early,* and he'd say, 'Because I just want to be with you, Daddy.'"

"Now every morning, when I park my car at work, I walk past that yellow school bus and cry."

Our heavenly Father desires our companionship, whether we think we need His or not. I'd like to suggest a reason for prayer and communion with heaven that goes beyond self-interest. The heart of God yearns for companionship with His children. You and I are His children. In my imagination I see Him looking at the yellow school bus and crying when we're not around.

God wants to give us more than things. He wants to give Himself! We pray because we are friends with God, and there is nothing holier. It is a bit of heaven on earth, a foretaste of what the saints are going to enjoy in glory.

Still, but Not Silent

Perhaps you're saying, "But the saints will *hear* Him talking back, and it's a whole lot easier to talk to someone who talks back. These monologues of mine are a little difficult sometimes. I suppose I should just be glad He's a good listener, because I never hear *Him* say anything."

No doubt, He does listen a whole lot more than He talks, but do you suppose He'd talk more if we'd be quiet long enough to hear Him speak? Psalm 46:10 says, "Be still, and know that I am God" (NIV).

Do you remember Elijah on the mountain? He was looking for God in the wind, then in an earthquake, and finally in fire, but he didn't find Him there. He went back into a cave and discovered that when God finally spoke, it was in a "still small voice" (1 Kings 19:12).

My preacher father once paid a visit to an elderly couple who were members of his congregation. Dad listened for some time as the woman spoke enthusiastically about many different subjects. Finally, during a momentary lull, her husband perked up with a question for my father. "Have you noticed my wife's speech impediment?" he asked.

"No," said my dad, "I haven't noticed her having *any* problem talking."

"She has to stop for breath," replied the old fellow.

Could it be that God would talk more if we would listen more? If we'd stop for longer breaths? The Bible premise is that God *wants* to talk to you! Are you aware of that? In John 15:15 Jesus says, "I have called you friends." Friends talk, don't they? What's important to us is important to them. Jesus is interested in what happens in your life. He cares. He's concerned about your joys and sorrows.

In John 14:21 He says, "I will love him, and *will manifest myself to him.*" What are some things that God would like to share with you? He'd like you to really *know* that He cares for you. He wants you to know that He understands about your pain, and suffering, and loneliness. He longs to give you peace. He'd like you to know that He wants more people to be with Him, and could use your help. He might even share with you that there have been some nasty lies spread about Him, and He needs your help to clear His name so that others might be attracted to Him also.

Hearing the Shepherd

What can we do to receive more of what He wishes to share? In John 10:2–5 Jesus says, "The man who enters by the gate is the shepherd of his sheep. The watchman opens the gate for him, and the sheep listen to his voice. He calls his own sheep by name and leads them out. When he has brought out all his own, he goes on ahead of them, and his sheep follow him because they know his voice. But they will never follow a stranger; in fact, they will run away from him because they do not recognize a stranger's voice" (NIV).

In John 10:14 Jesus continues, "I am the good shepherd; I know my sheep and my sheep know me" (NIV). I am struck by the fact that the sheep know His voice and that He calls them by name. If His sheep know His voice, then his voice would have to be *familiar* to them. They'd have to have heard it before. Sheep grow accustomed to the shepherd's voice by being *daily in his presence*. We need daily fellowship with the Good Shepherd if we're going to recognize His voice.

As we spend time with Jesus, we can learn to hear Him "speaking" and discover that He often uses nature, providential circumstances, music, people, Scripture, inspired reading material, and impressions in our own mind to communicate with us. An old song includes these lines:

> "When He calls me, I will answer.
> When He calls me, I will answer.
> When He calls me, I will answer.
> I'll be somewhere listening for my name.
> Oh I'll be somewhere listening,
> I'll be somewhere listening,
> I'll be somewhere listening for my name."

I'd like to consider some of the ways we can listen for the voice of Jesus through these various mediums of expression. But just before I do, let me put in a plug for journaling.

Journaling

Journaling could be described as keeping a diary of your prayers and God's responses. It can be done with a pen and notebook, typewriter, or computer. It can consist of sketchy notes and outlines, or lengthy paragraphs and pages. My own journal consists of rather brief notes that help me to remember conversations I have had during the time I reserve for prayer. I also record highlights of God's activity in my life from the previous day. I keep my journal on the computer and always include the date in the margin. Since I use a word processor, I have adopted the habit of italicizing messages that I believe come from Jesus so that I can quickly look back and spot meaningful dialogue.

One of the first concerns people have with journaling is the time it takes. But why would I not want to take time for communion with God? Talking with the King of the universe, who also happens to be my friend, will be one of the greatest privileges and joys of heaven. It certainly ought to be worth something *now*.

A second question could be: "Is slowing down to contemplate and write about spiritual things useful in helping me hear the 'still small voice'?" The answer is emphatically yes! In the midst of this maddening rush, God is speaking. But many, even in their seasons of devotion, fail to receive the blessing of real communion with God because they are in such great haste. With hurried steps they press through the circle of Christ's loving presence, pausing perhaps a moment but not waiting. They have no time to remain with the divine Teacher. We need more than just a pause for a moment in His presence. We need personal contact with Christ. We need to sit down in companionship with Him, and journaling s-l-o-w-s us down.

Journaling also brings other built-in benefits. You have a record of interaction with God that brings encouragement when read again later. (See Joshua 4:5-7.) We are far too quick to forget how God has led us in the past. We marvel when we're told of George Mueller's thousands of answered prayers. We probably have no fewer answers than he, but the difference between most of us and Mueller is that he kept a record of them. Because of the record, you also begin recognizing patterns of communication that God uses with you. A way that He communicates could go unnoticed if you hadn't written down a similar example on another occasion. But writing it down enables you to see it more clearly when it happens again.

There is no question that journaling takes time, but the rewards are more than worth the time and effort. And isn't the same true for just about anything else worth doing in life? Why should we balk at something that brings such blessing with God? Having said that, let's turn our attention to listening for God's "voice."

Nature

Recently I was troubled by a number of things that seemed overwhelming to me. I couldn't seem to stop worrying about them. I live by the Puget Sound where the tides rise and fall twice daily, and one day I found myself sitting on the shore talking with God about my concerns. I stopped talking for a while, and as I sat in stillness the thought was impressed upon me that the tides fall and rise with such precise regularity that accurate tide tables can be printed for hundreds of years forward or backward. I realized that God was dependable and that when we leave Him in charge, He never misses a beat. Peace rose like a tide in my heart as I clung to the God who holds all nature under His control.

For those who will pause and prayerfully look at the wonders of nature, the handwriting of nature's God will be readable and instructive. "When I consider your heavens, the work of your fingers, the moon and the stars, which you have set in place, what is man that you are mindful of him, the son of man that you care for him?" (Psalm 8:3, 4, NIV).

Providential Circumstances

Sometimes God communicates to us through situations and circumstances. A few years ago Marji was trying to decide if it were in God's plan for her to go back to college. Tuition for the class she was interested in was $300. Our finances were very tight, and we asked God to indicate His will by providing the money if she was to take the class. We came down to the final week of registration without having come up with any extra money and had almost concluded that Marji wasn't meant to take that class. Three days before registration ended, we received a $230 overpayment refund from our mortgage company. That was encouraging, but we were still $70 short. On the final morning of registration, God's message to Marji came in the form of a $100 check in the mail—sent by friends who said they had been impressed to give it to us, though they had no idea what it was needed for. We noted that the $330 total we had received gave us what we needed for tuition while leaving enough to return tithe to the God who sent it and had shown us that He was guiding our lives.

Proverbs 21:1 says, "The king's heart is in the hand of the Lord; he directs it like a watercourse wherever he pleases" (NIV). The same Lord who directs in the affairs of nations notes when a sparrow falls from its nest (see Matthew 10:29) and will certainly guide you as well. "In all your ways acknowledge Him, and He shall direct your paths" (Proverbs 3:6, NKJV).

Music

Many times I have heard God speaking to my heart or need through music. I will find myself humming a song whose lyrics contain a message perfectly matched to a situation or need in my life. The songs are not always sacred songs. One day, while desperate for counsel, I found myself singing a Carpenters song that says, "Let me be the one you run to, let me be the one you come to, when you need someone to turn to, let me be the one." It slowed me down and turned my heart toward Jesus.

On another occasion, after coming back from talking about the matchless charms of Jesus with a small group of fellow Christians, I found myself humming, "I Love to Tell the Story." As I contemplated the words I was moved by the appropriateness of their message.

> "I love to tell the story; for those who know it best
> Seem hungering and thirsting to hear it like the rest;
> And when in scenes of glory I sing the new, new song,
> 'Twill be the old, old story that I have loved so long."

Other times such songs come through the radio or my own CD

player as I listen to Christian music. I was able to share them just now because I had written them down in my journal and later found them, though I had already forgotten the experiences.

"He has put a new song in my mouth, a hymn of praise to our God. Many will see and fear and put their trust in the Lord" (Psalm 40:3, NIV).

People

God often communicates to us through Christian friends. Those who meet regularly with the body of Christ, at church or in home Bible fellowships, know how consistently they gather "meat in due season" while studying, praying, or sharing with other believers. All Christians have stories to tell of how God spoke to them through a friend's visit, phone call, letter, or note.

Three days ago I was concluding a week full of disappointments. It was a very low time for me, and I wondered how I would pull through. I kept asking God for affirmation and encouragement, but somehow I just couldn't seem to rise above the gloom and depression. Then I returned to my office after lunch and found two letters written by Christian friends who knew nothing of my discouragement but who couldn't have given more specifically needed encouragement.

I was extremely touched by God's kindness in prompting those notes, and I thanked Him profusely. But that wasn't the end. Later in the afternoon I received an exceptionally encouraging e-mail. When I got home that evening, Marji handed me another encouraging card that had been delivered to our mailbox. As if that hadn't been enough, God arranged for a group of friends to bring special encouragement to us the next morning—I guess to make good and sure that we we're well out of the mud. His message came through *loud* and clear!

Not only will God send you messages and encouragement through Christian friends; He will also speak to others through you. "Each one should use whatever gift he has received to serve others, faithfully administering God's grace in its various forms" (1 Peter 4:10, NIV).

Inspired Reading

In order for God to make use of this method of communication, it is helpful if you regularly read books and articles by Christian writers. Sometimes you will be amused by how pointedly God will speak to your situation; sometimes you will be amazed. A few weeks ago I was feeling as though it was past time for me to move to a new location of ministry. It seemed to me that my work in this pastorate had reached a point of wheel-spinning without much forward motion. I had told the Lord as much in prayer that morning, and then picked up *Imagine Meeting Him,* by Robert Rasmussen.

I opened to my bookmark and read an "imagined" letter from a disciple in Jerusalem writing to a friend about the futility of "waiting in Jerusalem," as Jesus had instructed following His resurrection. He complained that they had exhausted their effectiveness in that city, and speculated that remaining there seemed counterproductive to the gospel commission.

I chuckled to myself about the similarities to this piece of writing and my own prayers of that very morning. The "letter" continued to mirror my thoughts and feelings to its conclusion, and then I read the PS: "My friend, please disregard the above letter. I could not have been more wrong about waiting. Today was Pentecost. Am I glad that I am not in charge!"

Whoa! I thought. *Talk about receiving "meat in due season"! It hardly gets more relevant than that!* Once again God had met me where I was and offered me just the sort of encouragement I needed to continue in the journey.

"A word fitly spoken [or written] is like apples of gold in pictures of silver" (Proverbs 25:11). Have *you* read any good books lately?

Scripture

Probably the most dependable means for hearing God's voice is daily reading in His Word. Through His Word the Holy Spirit teaches, rebukes, encourages, and inspires us with messages from heaven. A current example from my life comes out of the discouraging circumstances I referred to earlier.

During a two-week span it seemed our family received more

knockdowns and incentives to discouragement than we had known in the past 10 years combined. In the midst of battle I sat down for some quiet time with God. I had been reading through the New Testament and "happened" to be in 2 Corinthians at the time. As I read chapter 4 that morning, the message from God was unmistakable.

"We are hard pressed on every side, but not crushed; perplexed, but not in despair; persecuted, but not abandoned; struck down, but not destroyed. . . . We who are alive are always being given over to death for Jesus' sake, so that his life may be revealed in our mortal body. . . . Therefore we do not lose heart. Though outwardly we are wasting away, yet inwardly we are being renewed day by day. For our light and momentary troubles are achieving for us an eternal glory that far outweighs them all. So we fix our eyes not on what is seen, but on what is unseen. For what is seen is temporary, but what is unseen is eternal" (verses 8-18, NIV).

I could have missed that wonderful word of encouragement if I were not in the custom of reading from God's Word on a daily basis. If you take time to open its pages regularly, you also will find messages from heaven that seem as if they had been sent 2,000 years ago to your address.

"Your word is a lamp to my feet and a light for my path" (Psalm 119:105, NIV).

Thoughts and Impressions

If you don't just fire off a prayer monologue and then run off to work, you may often find God speaking to you through thoughts and impressions in your mind as you wait quietly before Him.

One morning during my prayer time I said, "Lord, I really want to commune with You. I want to know Your voice like the sheep know the voice of the shepherd. So I'm going to try to listen, and I'm asking that You control my mind and enable me to hear You through the impressions and thoughts that You place in my head."

I told Him that I was going to write down whatever thoughts come into my mind and that I would assume that my thinking had been directed by Him.

I tried it, and there was no discernible thought to write. I remained quietly on my knees, with my eyes closed, waiting. Finally I said, "Well, Lord, either You aren't choosing to communicate or You're done, so I guess I'll say amen and go on my way."

The next morning I tried again, and this time I felt the impression *Pray for your friend Cary*. When that happened I said, "Where did that thought come from? I haven't thought of Cary for more than 10 years." But I wrote it down and dated the journal entry. It was just a thought. I didn't hear an audible voice. Two months later I received a phone call from Cary, who told me that his wife had nearly been killed in a horse accident. She had been in the hospital for weeks. I asked him when the accident had occurred, and began skimming through my journal, looking for the impression that had come to me. *It was the same day* that I had received the thought *Pray for your friend Cary*.

That was exciting to me; it told me I hadn't been confused. The impression had been from Jesus. I had taken the time to listen, and in the quiet He had communicated with me. Since then I've tried listening a whole lot more. Sometimes I get several impressions in one morning. Sometimes I get none, but I always try to write them down.

One morning I received the impression *to take Bob out for breakfast*. I said, "Lord, I don't know what I would talk about with that person." The next thought or impression that came into my mind (I wrote it down) was *I will show you what to say, and I will show you when. You just take him to breakfast.* (I wrote that down.)

I called the person that afternoon and said, "Can I take you to breakfast tomorrow morning?"

He said, "Why, sure! That would be nice." So we went to breakfast, and as I looked across the restaurant table I silently said, "Lord, You said You'd let me know what to say and when to say it. Please do. I'm waiting."

Abruptly Bob made a major shift in the conversation and jumped right to a place where it was appropriate for me to talk to him about his relationship with Jesus. I didn't initiate it! At that moment I felt a chill go down my spine. It was as if my angel whispered, "Now!"

I'm not claiming the gift of prophecy here. This is nothing spectacular. This is merely bread-and-butter stuff that any one of us can experience if we will just slow down long enough to listen for His voice.

"The sheep hear his voice; and he calls his own sheep by name and leads them out. And . . . he goes before them; and the sheep follow him, for they know his voice" (John 10:3, 4, NKJV).

I want to encourage you to listen to the Father. He wants to talk with you. Jesus *will* communicate with you *whenever* you pray, *wherever* you are, and *whatever* you're doing—if you just listen for His voice! He loves talking with His friends!

For Further Reflection
1. Prayer has been described as "the breath of the soul." List some lessons that can be derived from that metaphor for prayer.
2. Read a modern translation of Philippians 4:6, 7, reflecting on the following questions:
   a. What should you talk to God about?
   b. Is prayer a last-ditch effort, or a place to begin?
   c. What promise does God make to you through this passage?
3. Have you ever known someone who contacted you only when they wanted or needed something? How did you feel about their phone calls or visits?
4. Reflect on the following statement: We don't pray for "answers." *The answer is prayer!*
5. What encouragement can you receive from reading a modern translation of Romans 8:26?
6. Reflect on some instances when you felt that God communicated with you.
7. What are some things you can do to increase the likelihood of Psalm 46:10 being a reality for you?
8. In a practical sense, how can you apply the counsel found in 1 Thessalonians 5:16–18?

CHAPTER 6

Tell What You Know

$\mathcal{E}$ach of the four Gospels ends with a similar assignment. In the first Gospel Jesus says, "Go therefore and make disciples of all nations, baptizing them in the name of the Father and of the Son and of the Holy Spirit, and teaching them to obey everything that I have commanded you. And remember, I am with you always, to the end of the age" (Matthew 28:19, 20, NRSV). Why did Jesus leave us with these marching orders? Because He knows that inactivity results in atrophy.

Have you ever had a broken bone that was set in a cast? If you have, do you remember noticing how different your arm or leg looked when the cast was removed? Besides being lighter in color, it was smaller in size or circumference than the one that wasn't broken. The muscle had atrophied or shrunk, and it took exercise to get that arm or leg back to its former condition. Fortunately, as you were active and used that muscle, the muscle tone returned.

Mount Rainier

I live in the state of Washington. For nine years I was only 18 air miles from Mount Rainier National Park. The glaciers of this 14,411-foot volcano cause the mountain to stand out in bold relief as it dominates the landscape of Greater Seattle. Rainier has a magnetism that draws climbers from around the world, so I was excited when Jamie McPherson, a mountaineering friend of mine, offered to guide me to the top.

I told my wife I wanted to accept his offer, but she didn't think it was a good idea. I told her that it wasn't *dangerous,* since Jamie had all the right ropes and gear to negotiate any hazards safely. When she told me she wasn't concerned about the danger, I assured her that *cold* wouldn't be a problem either, since we both had parkas and would be climbing in July. She told me the *cold* wasn't why she didn't like the idea, so I asked if she was just jealous that she hadn't been invited also. "No," she said, "I don't have any desire to climb that mountain."

"Then what *is* the problem?" I asked.

"The problem *is,*" she said, "that you are 40 years old and haven't done any exercise since you were in college. No matter how fit Jamie is, he won't be able to *drag you* to the top. You are so out of shape you'll die up there."

I reminded her that I still weighed the same as I had in high school and told her that ought to count for something. But she said, "Weighing the same and being in shape are two different things. You might weigh the same, but you don't have the muscles you had 20 years ago."

I took that as a challenge, and a couple weeks later found myself struggling for breath as I toiled up the Muir snowfield on legs that seemed as dependable as spaghetti. Muir was the *easiest* part of the climb, and as we ascended I began taking almost as many rest stops as I took steps forward. I was so exhausted that when we crested the summit I collapsed in the snow and told Jamie I didn't even have enough energy left to make it to the summit register. I couldn't sign my name at the top. My failure to exercise over the years had made me a classic example of the axiom "Use it or lose it!" I had lost it.

Witness

In the Christian life "eating" has been compared to Bible study, "breathing" has been compared to prayer, and "exercise" has been compared to the Christian *witness.* Sharing Jesus with others is to your spiritual life what exercise is to your physical life. It is essential for spiritual health. To neglect the gospel commission is to invite spiritual feebleness and decay. Where there is no active labor for others, love for Jesus fades and faith grows dim.

I used the word *witness,* but we need a definition for it. Webster defines *witness* as: (1) testimony—something you have to say about someone or something; (2) the testimony of someone who saw and can give a firsthand report.

In other words, you must have witnessed something in order to *be* a witness. You can't witness unless you have seen or experienced a thing. Imagine someone who has never eaten chocolate trying to describe its taste. You have to have been a witness in order to give a firsthand report.

So what is the content of the Christian witness? What is the first-hand report? Consider the following scriptures and note their common denominator:

Psalm 66:16: "Come and hear, all of you who reverence the Lord, and I will *tell you what he did for me*" (TLB).

Daniel 4:2: "It is my pleasure to *tell you about the miraculous signs and wonders* that the Most High God has *performed for me*" (NIV).

John 3:11: "I tell you the truth, we speak of *what we know* and we testify to *what we have seen*" (NIV).

Acts 4:20: "We cannot stop telling about the wonderful *things we saw Jesus do and heard him say*" (TLB).

There is a big difference between explaining a theological doctrine and telling someone what God has done for you. One is *information;* the other is an *experience.* When we talk about sharing Jesus, we're talking about an experience. Jesus once told a group of church leaders, "You search the Scriptures, for in them you think you have eternal life; and these are they which testify of Me. But you are not willing to come to Me that you may have life" (John 5:39, NKJV). You see, there is something more to witnessing than simply telling people what the Bible teaches about a particular set of doctrines.

For example, I could probably give you 27 fundamental facts about the mayor of the town where I live. With a little research and a little help, I could probably give you his hat size, his shoe size, the color of his eyes, his home address, and an impressive list of other facts about him. But I have a friend who is the mayor's secretary. I'll venture to guess that she could tell us about him in a way that I couldn't, because she *knows him*. She spends time with him every day, so she could speak of him with a freshness and an insight that would capture the *man* and not just his shoe size.

There is a similar difference between what Josephus (the historian) wrote about Jesus and what John (the beloved disciple) wrote about Jesus. Josephus supplied a lot of information, but John told us what it was actually like to *be* with Jesus. In fact, John said it this way: "That which was from the beginning, which we have heard, which we have seen with our eyes, which we have looked at and our hands have touched—this we proclaim concerning the Word of life. The life appeared; we have seen it and testify to it. We proclaim to you what we have seen and heard, so that you also may have fellowship with us. And our fellowship is with the Father and with his Son, Jesus Christ" (1 John 1:1-3, NIV). The Christian witness, then, is a first-hand report about what it is like to have a friendship with Jesus.

God Benefits by Your Witness

In court a person on trial hopes to benefit by the testimony of the witnesses for the defense. The person hopes that as the defense witnesses are called, he or she will be exonerated. There is, because of His enemy's claims and charges, a sense in which God is on trial. In fact, Revelation 14:7 tells us that at the close of this earth's history, the "hour of his judgment is come." Many have thought that text referred to God judging *us,* but deeper study reveals the truth that *He* needs to be vindicated. There have been some terrible things said about God, and there are people on our planet who believe them. In addition, the enemy has been doing all he can to cause unfallen beings to have questions about God. God is on trial, and your witness can do some positive things for Him.

Jesus said, "Let your light [witness] so shine before men, that they may see your good works, and glorify your Father which is in heaven" (Matthew 5:16). One of the claims that God's enemy has made about Him is that He has unreasonable expectations—that His laws are impossible to keep. If you take a closer look at this verse, you discover that *God* gets glory from *your* good works. Why would people give glory to *God* if they were observing *your* good works?

If you go to Butchart Gardens in British Columbia and look at the beautiful flowers, you don't turn to people and say, "Wow! These are awesome daffodils! Can you believe the way they just grew here? Isn't it marvelous how they have arranged themselves in such wonderful patterns and combinations of color? If we were to buy some bulbs, I wonder if they would produce similar patterns in my yard." You don't praise the *flowers* at Butchart Gardens; you praise the *gardeners* who planted them in such wonderful patterns and combinations. *They* are the ones who get the praise.

If people are glorifying God because of the good works they see in you, they understand *who* is responsible for your Christlike life. They don't think that it is something you have done. They begin to see that God is able to re-create Himself in the lives of those who will submit to Him and spend time each day focusing on His matchless charms and goodness. You can be a witness for God's defense that disproves the enemy's claim that obedience is impossible.

In John 15:8 Jesus says, "This is to my Father's glory, that you bear much fruit" (NIV). Again, Jesus is showing how our lives can bring glory to His Father. As people see characteristics in us that are not natural to human nature, as they see us loving the "unlovable," forgiving our enemies, and being more interested in serving than in being exalted, they *know* a Higher Power had to make it happen. A transformed life brings glory to *God,* because even though some of us may produce external "goodness," none of us are capable of turning our *hearts* from evil. As it says in 2 Corinthians 4:7, "we have this treasure in jars of clay to show that this all-surpassing power is from God and not from us" (NIV). That's why *He* gets the glory.

Yet another text demonstrates that God benefits by your witness. Luke 18:43 says, "Immediately he received his sight and followed Jesus, praising God. When all the people saw it, they also praised God" (NIV). God looks good as people tell about what He has done for them.

First Peter 2:9 makes that clear again as Peter says, "You are a chosen generation, a royal priesthood, a holy nation, His own special people, that you may proclaim the praises of Him who called you out of darkness into His marvelous light" (NKJV). You have been given a task, a privilege, an opportunity to direct praise to God so that others might be attracted to Him. God wants more people to get in on this good news about friendship with Him, and our witness is useful in drawing others His direction.

Others Benefit by Your Witness

There is a benefit to others by our witness for God, but their *salvation* is not dependent upon our telling them the good news. Jesus didn't give the gospel commission because He needs us to help Him finish the work of telling humankind the salvation story. No. He can use other means than us to direct people to Himself. He has gone direct with visions, dreams, or even audible words when He chooses (see Genesis 15:1; Matthew 2:13; 1 Samuel 3:10). He has used angels (see 2 Kings 1:3). He has spoken through animals (see Numbers 22:28). In fact, Jesus once said that if the people were silent, the stones would cry out (see Luke 19:40).

Romans 9:28 says, "He will finish the work, and cut it short in righteousness: because a short work will the Lord make upon the earth." The Bible teaches that God doesn't need us to finish His work. No one will miss out on salvation because you or I failed to tell them about the Savior.

Imagine yourself ending up on the *outside* of the city of heaven, and one day during the final judgment you notice that your neighbor is on the *inside* of the city. You ask God why your neighbor made it and you didn't. Suppose He were to answer, "We owe you an apology for that. Your neighbor was supposed to have told you, but he dropped the ball, and we feel very bad about it. It really is unfortunate, and we hope you will try to understand." Would you be comfortable with that sort of explanation? I don't think so! I don't think the rest of the universe would be either.

John 1:9 says that Jesus is "the true Light which gives light to every man coming into the world" (NKJV). God is drawing every person to Himself, and He has made Himself responsible for giving every person an adequate chance to respond to His invitation.

So why *should* I tell others what Jesus means to me or what I mean to Him? Because while their salvation is not dependent upon my witness, that doesn't mean they receive no benefit from it. If you were hitchhiking to Philadelphia (the city of brotherly love) and I gave you a ride, you would get there more quickly, but you were going to get there sooner or later anyway. If you were hitchhiking to Las Vegas (the city of corruption) and I gave you a ride, you would get *there* more quickly, but you were going to get there sooner or later anyway.

Jesus is Lord, and He is determined to give you every opportunity to know Him—whether I help you or not. But my witness can help you get to know Him sooner! I can help you on your journey, and perhaps even spare you some trouble along the way. Further, the more I know Jesus, the more I *want* to help those He has invited to be heirs of salvation. So how does my witness benefit others?

John the Baptist, looking at Jesus as He walked by, said, "'Behold the Lamb of God!' . . . Two disciples heard him speak, and they followed Jesus" (John 1:36, 37, NKJV). People can hear what you say about Jesus and be attracted to Him sooner. This is good for them. It is something that we *want* for them! He is *worth* knowing, and we are eager for others to meet Him. When you are excited about or in love with someone, it is actually difficult *not* to speak about them.

According to John 1:40-42, "Andrew, Simon Peter's brother, was one of the two who heard what John had said and who had followed Jesus. The first thing Andrew did was to find his brother Simon and tell him, 'We have found the Messiah.' . . . And he brought him to Jesus" (NIV). Peter met Jesus sooner than he would have if his brother hadn't gone looking for him to share the good news.

The residents of Sychar "said to the woman [from the well], 'We no longer believe just because of what you said; now we have heard for ourselves, and we know that this man really is the Savior of the world'" (John 4:42, NIV). What happened here? She told them about Jesus, and because of what she said, they went to hear Him for themselves. *They* became involved in a personal experience with Jesus and thanked the woman for introducing them to Him. They received real benefit from her witness.

Jesus Himself said, "And I, when I am lifted up from the earth, will draw all people to myself" (John 12:32, NRSV). If you lift Him up, people are attracted to what they see. They too want to come and know Him better. There are *fantastic* benefits to others when you lift Jesus up before them.

I'll never forget a gentleman in his 60s who had spent a lifetime trying to please God by working desperately on rule-keeping and behavior. He had just understood, for the first time, that Christianity is about who you know, not about what you do. Tears fell from his eyes as he told me of the burden that had dropped away. "It is the best news I have never heard," he said. "It is too good to be true." Praise Jesus that it *is* true, and that others always benefit from hearing that news!

You Benefit by Your Witness

Are you aware of the principle that while seeking to help others we actually help ourselves more? The most miserable people in the world are the ones who live only for themselves.

Those who do nothing but pray will soon cease to pray, or their prayers will become a formal routine. When Christians stop working earnestly for the Master, who worked earnestly for them, they lose much of the subject matter of prayer and have no hunger or thirst for time alone with God. Their prayers become self-centered.

The Spring

High in the Colorado Rockies my parents owned a redwood cabin sitting on a parcel of land surrounded by national forest. Our family affectionately referred to it as The Property.

We first visited The Property in April. While exploring, we came across a grove of aspen trees surrounded by ferns and tall grass. The soil was dark and damp. Wondering if digging would uncover a spring, we got tools from the cabin and prepared to find out.

We soon had a hole carved into the mountainside—a distorted circle about four feet across and two feet deep. The soil became more damp with each shovelful of earth we removed. Gradually the dampness changed to mud. Finally water bubbled up.

The puddle that formed was muddy. It seeped in so slowly that we decided to leave it alone for a while. After a couple hours we were delighted to find the hole two-thirds full of cold, clear water. We took a drink and left, hoping that when we returned it would be full and overflowing.

Imagine our disappointment two hours later when we discovered the water level to be exactly the same as it had been earlier. We pondered the mystery and wondered why it had stopped filling. We probed about the bottom to see if the seep spots had gotten clogged or covered, but we only made the water muddy again.

We wondered if the pressure on the bottom had increased (as the hole filled) to the point where it could no longer seep. To test that theory, we took an old pipe and pushed it through the soil from the downhill side. It penetrated our reservoir below the water line, acting as a drain.

We watched as the reservoir drained lower and lower. Finally it reached the top of the drainpipe. Then an amazing thing happened. Water kept draining out, but the water line remained constant at the top of the drainpipe! We kept waiting for the water to stop draining, but it never happened. In amazement we watched a steady stream continue pouring from the end of the drainpipe.

We ran and got a six-gallon container from the cabin. Placing the container beneath the stream of water, we clocked the rate of fill with a stopwatch. We couldn't believe the results! The little "seeps" we had uncovered in the ground were producing water at the rate of three gallons per minute! We were pleased and drank deeply.

Later that year we returned to The Property in late October for another visit. The aspen leaves had turned to gold, falling like nuggets to the ground. I went for a walk in the forest and decided to check the spring. I was disappointed to find no water coming out of the pipe. The once-clear water had become murky and stagnant, with tiny insects swimming about.

At first I thought it was simply because the water source had dried up. Then I noticed leaves and debris clogging the outlet. Reaching through the muck, I cleared the drain. Water began flowing once again, and before I left for home that week, the spring was clear.

Nature demonstrated this spiritual principle: *As you share what you know and love about Jesus, you will receive more to share. Activity is the very condition of life! Your experience with Him will continue fresh and new as you "spill over" with the good news each day. If you don't "let it out," what was once new will become old, stagnant, and undesirable.*

The reason Jesus gave the gospel commission to human beings instead of angels is that He knows it is good for *us* to be active for Him. If you will become involved for Jesus, you will feel the need of a deeper experience with Him. *Your* faith will be strengthened, *your* soul will drink deeper drafts at the well of salvation. *You* will get more out of Bible study and prayer. *You* will grow in grace and in the knowledge of Christ, and *you* will develop a rich experience.

More Time With Jesus

There is another personal benefit for you when you share Jesus with others. It is the greatest benefit of all. It has to do with Jesus. Would you like to spend *more* time with Jesus? When you consider His life, what do you see Him doing most? Jesus' favorite pastime is looking for lost people. This gives new meaning to Luke 11:23, where Jesus said, "Whoever is not with me is against me, and whoever does not gather with me scatters" (NRSV).

If you could have been with Jesus through history, what would you have spent most of your time doing?

You would have run to catch up with Him as He followed Adam and Eve out of the Garden of Eden to tell them some good news about rescue. You would have been there as He caught up with fugitive Jacob at Bethel, and with Moses by a burning bush.

You would have seen Him for 40 years in a cloud during the day and a fireball at night as He stayed with unbelieving Israel in the wilderness. You'd have seen Him standing between the pillars with Samson, just before the roof came down.

You would have followed as He chased Jonah into the hold of a ship and then into the belly of a whale. You would have felt the heat as He saved three guys from a fiery furnace—or the cold of night, as He protected Daniel from a den of lions.

You would have walked 50 miles with Him, from Galilee to Tyre and Sidon, to save a troubled mother's daughter from the evil one. You would have walked 25 miles with Him, from Jordan to Bethany, to comfort two grieving sisters and rescue their brother from the grave.

You would have joined "Jesus the Good Samaritan" as He ministered to the wounded and the dying. You would have joined "Jesus the Good Shepherd" as He left 99 sheep to go find one lost in darkness. You would have joined Him and the woman, who was looking for a coin that was lost in the house. You would have worked another year with Him for an orchard tree condemned to destruction.

You would have seen Him cleanse 10 lepers from their loathsome disease. You would have heard Him tell a paralyzed man that his sins were forgiven. You'd have seen Him save a prostitute—and then transform her into the first herald of the resurrection.

You would have seen Him rescue a dying thief while *He* was suffering superhuman agony. You would have seen Him running after Saul on the Damascus road.

You'd see Him knocking today on your neighbor's door, seeking entrance. You'd join Him in hospital halls and beside patient beds. You'd listen with Him to the aged in retirement centers and convalescent hospitals. You'd join Him in welcoming strangers into the family of Christ.

If you want to hang around with Jesus, you'll get a lot more of His time if you're willing to look for lost people who would like to find their way home.

What Does a Witness Say?

Three of the Gospel writers tell the story of two demoniacs whom Jesus set free. The deliverance cost some ranchers a herd of pigs, and they were so upset about their losses that they asked Jesus to get out of town. He turned to leave, but as He was stepping back into the boat that had brought Him there, the restored demoniacs fell at His feet and begged to go with Him. Jesus responded to theirs request by saying, "Go home to your own [family and relatives and friends] and bring back word to them of how much the Lord has done for you, and [how He has] had sympathy for you and mercy on you" (Mark 5:19, Amplified).

The restored demoniacs had been privileged to hear the teachings of Jesus for a only a few moments. "Not one sermon from His lips had ever fallen upon their ears. They could not instruct the people as the disciples who had been daily with Christ were able to do. But they bore in their own persons the evidence that Jesus was the Messiah. They could tell what they knew; what they themselves had seen, and heard, and felt of the power of Christ. This is what everyone can do whose heart has been touched by the grace of God. . . . As witnesses for Christ, we are to tell what *we know, what we ourselves have seen and heard and felt.*" If we have been spending time with Jesus, we will have "something right to the point to tell concerning the way in which He has led us. We can tell how we have tested His promise, and found the promise true. We can bear witness to what we have known of the grace of Christ. This is the witness for which our Lord calls, and for the want of which the world is perishing" (*The Desire of Ages,* p. 340).

You don't have to be a professional to tell what you know of Jesus. All you need to do is *know Jesus* and what He has done for you. Then tell a friend! You'll be the one who receives the greatest blessing. Could anyone be lost if you don't witness? Yes! *You.*

For Further Reflection
1. Make a spiritual application from the fact that the fresh, life-sustaining waters of the Sea of Galilee have an outlet, while the briny, lifeless waters of the Dead Sea have no outlet other than evaporation.
2. Expand on lessons that can be learned from the fact that witnessing is to spiritual health what exercise is to physical health.
3. Give a personal example that demonstrate the truth of the expression "use it or lose it."
4. Why is somebody more likely to be spiritually influenced by your personal testimony than by your expert defense of Bible truth?
5. Based on Jesus' "marching orders" in Mark 5:19, what should be our first line of business regarding *strangers* with whom we

wish to share the gospel?

6. Summarize each of the following verses in your own words. Then write a definition for witnessing based upon the conclusions they lead you to.

        Psalm 66:16
        Daniel 4:2
        John 3:11
        Acts 4:20

7. What is perhaps the most recurring thread in 1 John 1:1-3?

8. How can sharing (1) what Jesus is to you and (2) what you are to Him benefit you in the following areas?

        Making your life an adventure
        Providing real purpose for living
        Building your spiritual confidence
        Increasing your understanding and appreciation of Jesus.

CHAPTER 7

Who Wants to Fight?

In his poem "The Ballad of Salvation Bill," Robert Service tells the story of a Yukon fur trapper who rescues a nearly frozen missionary. They end up stranded together in a small cabin as winter storms make travel impossible. The chain-smoking trapper becomes desperate after finding that his cigarette paper has been chewed up by mice. During a nicotine fit he threatens and begs the preacher to let him use the pages of his Bible to roll tobacco into cigarettes. At first the horrified preacher refuses, but finally he consents after making Bill promise to read each page before he smokes it. The following excerpt describes the result.

> And so I did. I smoked and smoked
>   from Genesis to Job,
> And as I smoked I read each blessed word;
>   While in the shadow of his bunk
>   I heard him sigh and sob,
> And then . . . a most peculiar thing occurred.
>   I got to reading more and more,
>   and smoking less and less,
> Till just about the day his heart was broke,
>   Says I: "Here, take it back, me lad.
>   I've had enough, I guess.
> Your paper makes a mighty rotten smoke."

Make a note of this: Bill found his behavior changing *naturally* as he spent time with God. He made no resolutions, he set no goals, he attempted no reforms, but he experienced a radical change. Does this happen only in poems or stories?

If you are like me, you have probably not done well at keeping New Year's resolutions. I've had such poor success that I *resolved* a few years ago not to make any more resolutions at New Year's. Have you ever tried to use sheer grit and determination to make yourself a better person? If you're like the 90 percent of us who don't have enough backbone, then you have discovered that all of your promises and resolutions are like ropes of sand.

I'd like to suggest that the backboned 10 percent who *can* do what they resolve are in just as much trouble as those who can't—if they don't know Jesus for themselves. In fact, they are in deeper trouble, because Jesus said that those who think they're healthy are not likely to spend much time with the Great Physician (see Mark 2:17). People who feel a great need are the most likely to come to Jesus for healing. Those who stay away are sick, even though they may appear healthy.

Incentive to Discouragement

I believe that one of the biggest reasons people give up on a personal relationship with Jesus is that they become discouraged with failures in their life. There's hardly anything more frustrating than wanting victory over weaknesses and not getting it.

After I first became a Christian, I read everything I could find on the life of Jesus, and my relationship with Him grew for about two years. Then I began to get discouraged with failure and what appeared to me to be a lack of progress in overcoming some specific weaknesses in my life. I felt convicted that these problem areas *ought* to be out of my life. I would pray for victory, and struggle for victory, and seek victory. I desperately wanted to be an overcomer, but I just kept failing and falling.

I became very discouraged because every time I failed, the devil would whisper in my ear, "You must not really be a Christian. If you *were,* you wouldn't keep doing this. This relationship, this quiet time, this starting your day with Jesus, is not making any difference for you. You might as well give it up. You're still falling. You're no better now than when you started this relationship. Yes-s-s-s," the snake hisses, "you might as well give it up!"

I began to feel so ashamed of my failures that I would stay away from Jesus. I felt embarrassed to go to Him after failing. I would let time go by before I prayed or read or spent any time with Him. I would try hard not to do the thing that I had failed at, and if I could manage five or six days of good behavior, I would come to Jesus and ask for forgiveness. I thought that my six days of good behavior proved I was sincere and made Him more willing to take me back. I figured I'd earned a little bit of grace (as if you can).

The mother of a soldier once came to Napoleon to appeal her son's sentence of execution for falling asleep while on duty. She asked that Napoleon would extend grace to her boy.

Napoleon replied, "He doesn't deserve grace."

"If he deserved it," answered the mother, "it wouldn't be grace."

Grace is *unmerited* favor, but somehow I thought that if I could go along for a few days without blowing it, then I would be more worthy to come into Jesus' presence. This type of thinking is a strange paradox when you consider that what Jesus is most interested in is *fellowship* and *communion* with us. Since the real issue in sin is *not* doing bad deeds but rather neglecting Jesus as your friend, then staying away from Him until you've had a few days of "good behavior" is actually hurting Him more than the bad behavior that caused you to stay away. His heart is broken more by your remaining away than by the thing you did! In fact, the "failure" was not sin; *staying away is!*

He loves spending time with us, and He knows that we are never going to stop our bad behavior unless *He* changes us. He also knows that He can't change us (from the inside out) unless we keep spending time with Him. So staying away from Jesus because we feel guilty, ashamed, embarrassed, or discouraged with our failures is the worst thing we can do for ourselves. *And* it brings the greatest pain to Jesus.

The Great Divide
People who struggle to overcome and to be victorious generally

fall into one of two camps. Either they decide that obedience is impossible and therefore unimportant, *or* they give up Christianity
completely. After two years of spending daily time with Jesus, I became so discouraged with my failures that I quit seeking to know
Him at all.

I felt so ashamed and guilty for coming back to Him time after
time with my failures that I decided it would be better to stop coming. At that point I made a deliberate choice to quit spending time
with Him. I wasn't interested in wild or wicked rebellion; I just
didn't want to have a relationship with Jesus anymore. I decided to
try to cruise along in neutral, not realizing that there really is no spiritual middle ground. I had forgotten that Jesus said, "He that is not
with me is against me" (Matthew 12:30).

I wasn't *with* Him. I gave up seeking to know Him better each
day. Two more years passed as I lived my life apart from Jesus. Then
one day it occurred to me that my life was at a much lower point than
when I had let go of Jesus. (When you coast, you don't go uphill.)

Miraculously, something began to penetrate my thick skull.
While in the relationship with Jesus I had felt as though I could see
no measurable growth in my life, but after neglecting Him for two
years I realized that I would give anything to be where I used to be
back at the place I was when I'd given up.

We are the last people who should be taking our own spiritual
temperature! Jesus never made you or me a fruit inspector. Like a
child who keeps digging up seeds to see if the plants are growing,
our personal inspections are counterproductive. Jesus doesn't ask us
to look at ourselves and our imperfections. Instead He says, "Come
unto me, . . . and I will give you rest" (Matthew 11:28).

Another way many Christians deal with their failures is to say
that it doesn't really matter how one lives. Their line of reasoning
goes something like this: *Because we are all sinners, we are going to fail
and fall until Jesus comes. Don't worry about your imperfections; just be
thankful for the cross and forgiveness. Someday, when He comes the
second time, we will all be changed "in a moment, in the twinkling of an
eye" (1 Corinthians 15:52). However, until then failure is inevitable, so
don't worry about it.*

That was unacceptable to Keith. Keith struggled with homosexuality. He didn't want to be gay, but try as he might, he couldn't seem to change his sexual orientation. Finally, seeking help, he confided his problem to his pastor. The pastor told him that he could expect to fail and fall until Jesus came again, but that he should not despair because, since Calvary, forgiveness is available for every sin. Kevin tried to be thankful for forgiveness and live with failure for four more years. Finally, however, he decided that the Second Coming was too far away, and he ended his life by carbon monoxide poisoning.

I once saw a bumper sticker that said, "God accepts you just the way you are . . . but He loves you too much to leave you that way." A transformed life *must* be a real possibility, or Jesus wouldn't have talked four times as much about obedience, victory, and overcoming as He did about forgiveness. Is the solution just to try harder to live a Christlike life? Is that what is missing? More willpower and determination?

No Money Down

Most Christians believe we are forgiven and *saved by faith,* not by our own works of obedience. Yet most of those same people seem to think that once we are forgiven, we spend the remainder of our Christian lives trying hard to perfect Christlike characters. They have exchanged the burden of salvation for the burden of holiness, working hard to prove by "right living" that they really do appreciate the gift of forgiveness.

Let me ask you a question. If I came to you and said, "I will give you any car you want for no money down," how would you respond? I suspect you would want to know if there were any monthly payments, right? If I told you the payments would be $1,200 a month for the rest of your life, would you want one of those cars? It probably wouldn't take you long to say, "No, thanks!"

Is that what we are doing with salvation? Do we say "Salvation is a free gift. You don't have to do a thing to be forgiven. Just come to Jesus as you are, tell Him that you want Him to be Lord of your life, and ask Him to forgive you for the years you have neglected

Him. BUT once you become a Christian, you will have to work your tail off trying to act like and remain one"? Is that what we're saying? The down payment is free, but the monthly payments will kill you off? What sort of gift is that?

I was once given (free) a registered Irish setter puppy that was the pick of the litter. It was the worst and most expensive gift I have ever received. I had more trouble with that dog than you could shake a stick at! I had vet bills, dog-catcher bills (he kept running off), and expenses galore to replace or repair things he had damaged. He cost me more in pain, sleeplessness, time, and money than any other gift I've ever received! I came to the point where I felt like saying, as Mark Twain once did: "If the . . . funeral [of the one responsible for giving me the animal] took place, I would postpone all other recreations and attend it."

If someone offers you the free gift of salvation, but leaves you with the burden of holiness, they haven't done you a favor. This leaves us with a dilemma. If ignoring our failures is not the answer, and if giving up Christianity doesn't fix anything, what can we do?

Who Helps Whom?

There is a third alternative. Philippians 2:13 says, "It is God who is at work in you, enabling you both to *will* [that relates to your desires, your choices, the longings of your heart) and to *work* [that relates to your actions] for his good pleasure" (NRSV). Did you notice who does *both?* God does both!

He doesn't say, "Look, you do your part, and I'll do the rest, for of course you know that *I help those who help themselves."* Those aren't God's words; they have been attributed to Aesop, and later were written by Benjamin Franklin in *Poor Richard's Almanac.* They have been quoted as though they were Scripture for hundreds of years, and it is my opinion that "an enemy hath done this" (Matthew 13:28).

The truth is, God helps those who realize that they *cannot* help themselves. In fact, every time human beings try to help God do something that God promised to do for them, they mess things up. Do you remember Abraham and the child of promise? Do you recall Jacob and the birthright? The Bible is full of people who tried to do what God promised to do for them. Whatever God promised to do for you, you had better not try to do, because you will only mess it up! If He *doesn't* promise to do it for you, you better be attentive and participate. And He never promised to fight the "fight of faith" for you.

The good news is that God promises to fight the fight of sin *for* you if you will "fight the good fight of faith" (1 Timothy 6:12). Faith is the same as trust. In order to trust somebody who is completely trustworthy, all I have to do is get to know them. Therefore, the "fight of faith" would be the effort to get better acquainted with Jesus. Restated: The "fight of faith" is the fight to come daily into His presence for the purpose of fellowship and communion. That's the real fight! And those who think that that is not a fight are people who haven't tried doing it.

Those who maintain that "good works" are the natural *result* of developing a personal friendship with Jesus are often accused of promoting a do-nothing religion. To such, I would say, "Excuse me? You must have never tried this!" At times it will take every ounce of willpower you possess to come into His presence. But if you use your power of choice to do *that,* He will do the rest!

God wants to change our hearts. He wants to give us transplants and power to obey. The good news is that He's interested in giving us the car with no money down, *and* He wants to make the monthly payments. That's a gift and a friend that you don't want to walk away from!

Both Will and Do?

How does it happen? Colossians 2:6 says, "As you therefore have received Christ Jesus the Lord, so walk in Him" (NKJV). You walk the Christian life in the same way you become a Christian. How do you "receive" Christ? Jesus said, "This is eternal life, that they may know You, the only true God, and Jesus Christ whom You have sent" (John 17:3, NKJV). You receive Christ, or become a Christian, by getting to know Jesus. Right? If that's how you become a Christian, then how you continue in the Christian life is by becoming even *better* acquainted with Him. Life eternal is based on knowing Him, and a life of obedience is the result of continuing to know Him on a daily basis. "As you received, so walk . . . "

According to Romans 1:17, "the just [justified] shall *live by faith*" also. Remember, as Jesus dwells in us, He promises to work in us "both to will and to do of his good pleasure." God wants to change not only our actions (which would be *doing*) but also our desires (which would be *willing*). *Remember,* He does both. You do neither.

If you think you do, sooner or later you will become discouraged, or you will have a false sense of security based upon substituting willpower for righteousness.

Badness held in check is not goodness! Those who think so are overlooking Jeremiah 13:23, which reminds us that we are no more able to produce "heart" goodness than a leopard is able to remove its spots. If God looks at the heart (see 1 Samuel 16:7), then I am in trouble, because the only righteousness I can produce is like filthy rags (see Isaiah 64:6)! That is why both *willing* and *doing* have to be His department.

Just a Minute . . .

There are those who protest at this point, "What about James 4? Doesn't he write that we are to 'resist the devil'? Sounds like something for us to do if we want him to flee from us." Let's take a closer look at that scripture: "Submit yourselves therefore to God. Resist the devil, and he will flee from you. Draw near to God, and he will draw near to you" (James 4:7, 8, NKJV).

Please notice the three-sentence-sandwich here. Before "resisting" is even mentioned, we are instructed to "submit yourselves to God." On the other side of "resisting," we are once again encouraged to "draw near to God," with the promise that as we do that, "he will draw near to you." "Resisting the devil" is like a thin slab of American cheese pressed between two *relationship* pieces of bread.

According to the Greek professor where I attended college, these verses are actually saying that our part in resisting the devil is to draw near to God. As we surrender (submit) moment by moment to Him and come into a closer relationship with Him (draw near), He takes control of the battle, and the devil flees.

I am glad that He wants to fight for me, because I've tried plenty of gimmicks without success. During my years of being discouraged with my failures, I tried all sorts of things. People told me about "warfare prayer," hymn singing during temptation, counting to 10, and verse quoting, ad nauseum. I tried each new gimmick with no success.

I was told that Jesus, in His wilderness temptations, overcame the devil by quoting Scripture. I don't think so! I believe that Jesus quoted Scripture because He was so familiar with it. And He was so familiar with it because His habit was to rise up "a great while before day," go out "into a solitary place," and pray (see Mark 1:35).

Jesus was committed to building the relationship with His Father by taking time for fellowship and communion with Him each day. He would "draw near" and "surrender" to the Father, and the dependent, submissive relationship that Jesus had with His Father is what carried Him through in the wilderness. The power that sent the devil scampering came from heaven, not from Jesus.

Our problem is that we tend to depend on *our* (imagined) power instead of *His*. We take cold showers. We try to redirect our minds and think of something other than the temptation. We try carrying a pocket New Testament, thinking there is some sort of magic in having the Bible physically with us. We try commanding Satan to leave, or ordering him to "get behind" us, only to discover that once he is there, he seems to push.

Two Problems

There are two major problems with this kind of approach to obedience, victory, and holiness. The first problem is that *staying out of trouble does not constitute a changed heart.*

I once asked a group of people, "If I want to hit you, but I choose not to, is that a true victory?"

A huge, muscular fellow in the audience stood and bellowed out, "You bet!"

I replied with emphasis, "If I *want* to hit you, but I don't, is *that* a true victory?"

"You better believe it!" he answered.

I said, "I'd like to suggest that it isn't a *true* victory, and I'm wondering if we could talk later—after I've had a chance to finish."

"Fair enough," he said, and sat back down so I could continue. After the meeting, he came up and told me that he was an ex-marine who had cultivated a love for violence. He said he actually found pleasure in feeling someone's bones crunching beneath his fist.

"Let me tell you, buddy," he said as he towered above me. "If I *want* to hit you, and I *don't* hit you, I call it a victory!"

"Amen, brother," I quickly responded. "Amen!"

But is that *really* a victory? We already noted that our hearts are evil and we cannot change them (see Jeremiah 13:23). If my heart is not changed and I still want to do the thing that I am not doing, is that victorious Christian living? Is that what God calls obedience?

There are real advantages to avoiding evil even though your heart is attracted to it. It can keep you out of jail, it can keep your reputation from becoming tarnished, it can lessen the damage you cause to others, but it is not righteousness and it is not victory. As we said earlier, badness held in check is not goodness.

The second problem is that *fighting the battle at the point of temptation is fighting the battle at the wrong location.*

During World War II, the Allies placed fake plans for attack on the body of a dead airman and left him floating off enemy shores. The Germans found the "plans" and moved their troops to defend the location mentioned in them. The Allies then entered several undefended locations; it was considered a turning point in the war.

When you fight the battle at the wrong location, you end up losing the war. If I am trying to fight sin by trying to stop doing bad things, I'm fighting the battle at the wrong location.

Remember, the real issue in sin is not a *behavior* issue; it's a *relationship* issue. Romans 14:23 reminds us that "whatsoever is not of faith is sin," and faith (or trust) presupposes a relationship with the person or object trusted.

In chapter 2 we noted that even good deeds, apart from a personal, daily relationship with Jesus, are considered bad deeds by Him. Jesus' stories in Matthew 7 and Luke 13 demonstrate that the real issue in sin and salvation is not what I do, but whom I know. Do you know Jesus? The question is *not:* "Are you doing good, or are you doing better at behaving than you were yesterday?" No! The question of importance is: "Are you becoming better acquainted with Jesus today than you were yesterday? Are you growing in knowing Him?"

A Little Math

Let's consider the following two texts: In John 15:5 Jesus said, "Without Me you can do nothing" (NKJV). How much is nothing? Zero? Nothing is what you have left after you *peel* a zero! Apart from Jesus you and I can do *nothing*. If we were to try to illustrate that mathematically, it might look like this:

$$Y(you) - X(Christ) = 0 \text{ (nothing)}$$

Is that *really* true? Can't we produce some right actions? Perhaps, but actions are external, and God looks at our hearts, which we've already noticed we are powerless to change.

Now look at Philippians 4:13: "I can do *all* things through Christ who strengthens me" (NKJV). Mathematically, that could be represented this way:

$$Y(you) + X(Christ) = 4(infinity)$$

In the first equation, nothing gets done. In the second, everything is accomplished. The only difference between the two equations is X (Christ). The presence of Jesus makes all the difference! If without Him I can do nothing but with Him I can do everything, who is doing the "all things" that are being done? *Jesus!* Not me! *He* is doing it through me. So what is left for me to do? *Get With Jesus* every day!

He says, "I'll *transform* your heart if you'll give Me the opportunity. I'll change it. In fact, I will give you a *new* heart" (see Ezekiel 36:26). "Come to me, all you who are weary and burdened," He says in Matthew 11:28, "and I will give you rest" (NIV). Coming to Him is all about relationship building—getting to know Jesus, the source of rest.

A Closer Look at an Eternal Principle

Second Corinthians 3:18 tell us that by beholding we become changed. That is true in both a negative and a positive way. If I behold my failures even though it is for the purpose of overcoming them, *they* have my attention. If my prayers are focused on asking Jesus to help me overcome my weaknesses, there is danger that I'm not seeking Him for His sake, but for victory over failure. My attention will be primarily upon myself and my weaknesses. I will find the beholding-we-become-changed principle working negatively and making me more like the very thing I am trying to overcome. My attention is in the wrong direction.

What is a positive application of the beholding principle? If I want to become more like Jesus, what do I need to behold? Simple answer: Jesus. Not my failures—even for the purpose of getting rid of them.

If you will seek Jesus for Jesus' sake, and not for victory, victory will be given as an extra. Jesus is more interested in your friendship than He is in your performance. He knows that if you and He become better and better friends, your performance will change as a natural result of that relationship. *You* won't work on it, but it *will* change.

When I write a check at a store and a merchant accepts it, that merchant is assuming that I've made a deposit in the bank at an earlier time to cover the amount of the check. If you want to fight the fight of *faith,* instead of the fight of *sin,* then you need to make deposits in your relationship checking account. The way you do that is by spending time with Jesus every day, becoming better acquainted with Him. Remember the formula? *Time alone at the beginning of every day in contemplation of the life of Jesus, through His Word and through prayer.* As you spend time with Jesus, your checking account of grace and power continues to grow, and when the enemy "comes in like a flood" (see Isaiah 59:19). the Banker raises up a standard against him. He says, "I've got you covered," and writes a check that sends the devil scampering.

Transformed by Love

When I was in college, I did not get along with people who

worked on security. I called them vege cops and had frequent conflicts with them. They seemed to be people who for some reason felt the need to wield power as a means of getting even for injustices they had suffered during childhood. I strongly resented and resisted their assumed authority over me and did what I could to make their job difficult.

I would dutifully park my car in "reserved" spaces, and they would dutifully leave citations under my windshield wipers. I would let the citations build up on my windshield, without paying them, until the rainy season arrived. Then I would use my wipers to scatter the tickets across campus like the leaves of autumn.

On one occasion I led them in a high-speed chase around the third floor of the men's dormitory. I was on a motorcycle, and that high crime did little to endear me to campus security.

One day the ongoing tension between us led to a confrontation in the street. While on patrol, they spotted my Datsun station wagon parked on a city street in front of a school-owned home. As a crowd gathered round, two officers and I got into a high-volume discussion regarding my rights and their authority, which ended with me leaving them humiliated as *I* drove *their* patrol car away.

The next day I was called in by the dean of student affairs, who told me I was to make a public apology for what I had said and done to the two security officers the day before. When I told him I wasn't sorry, he informed me that *that* was not the issue and that if I desired to continue as a university student, an apology would be required. He concluded our conversation by giving me a day to consider the matter seriously and take the appropriate action.

I left his office determined that I would transfer to another university before I would apologize. For some reason, however, he didn't follow through, and I ended up remaining a student there—without having to say I was sorry.

Shortly after this I fell in love with Marji, a girl who I later found out worked for security! (She had been undercover when I met her.) Too late, I learned where she worked—and I suffered the serious embarrassment of having fallen in love with an officer.

One Saturday night I was keeping her company while she

worked the "dispatcher shift" in the office. Foolishly I turned the conversation to all the reasons I did not like people who worked on security (present company excluded, of course) and particularly began deriding the two officers I had been told to apologize to. I said nasty, rotten things that I am ashamed to write, and as I was talking, I heard throats clearing in the room on the other side of an open door. I looked up to see the very two guys I was talking about!

They had heard it all, and I became suddenly speechless, feeling much like the kid caught with his hand in the cookie jar. I looked at Marji. She didn't say a word. We watched them walk across the room and leave without speaking. I looked again at Marji and noticed tears rolling down her cheeks. With broken voice she said, "Regardless of how you feel about those guys, I have worked with them for three years, and they've been special friends to me. It really hurts to know that what you said brought pain to people I care a lot about."

Then an amazing thing happened! Suddenly wild horses couldn't have kept me from apologizing to those officers. I drove until I found them and asked their forgiveness for being such a jerk. I told them there was no excuse for my bad attitude or caustic behavior. I offered my hand and asked for a chance to start over. All of my negative feelings toward those guys had vanished!

I did not *work* at that apology. I did not say, "I really *ought* to do this in order to have a better relationship with Marji," or "I need to do this if I value my relationship with Marji," or "I don't *want* to do this, but I *will.*" NO! It was not hard to apologize. In fact, it would have been harder for me *not* to apologize! What made the difference? Love! Love can enable you to do things naturally that otherwise couldn't even be forced. Do you see why building your friendship with Jesus is so important? Do you see how He uses love to transform us?

He promises that if He is lifted up, He will draw all men, women, and children to Himself (see John 12:32). As you spend daily time getting to know Jesus better, you will find yourself being drawn to Him. You will appreciate Him more and more. You will find love in your heart for Jesus that wasn't there before you began spending time communicating with Him for friendship's sake.

As this love and friendship grows, when you discover that some-thing you are doing brings pain to your Friend, you will find your-self loath to repeat it. You won't have to say, "I choose to do the right thing, regardless of how I feel," because you won't *want* to do wrong. Jesus promises to take the unhealthy *desires* away. When you fight the battle at the right location, one day you'll discover that the war is won! You've been *given* the victory!

That's why Paul considers "everything a loss compared to the surpassing greatness of knowing Christ Jesus" (Philippians 3:8, NIV) And Paul can promise in Philippians 1:6 that "he who began a good work in you will carry it to completion by the day of Christ Jesus" (NIV). Because *He* does good work!

For Further Reflection

1. Do the following texts fill you with hope and courage? Why?
     Matthew 5:48
     Romans 7:15-24
     2 Corinthians 7:1
2. In a battle, before you can know *how* to fight, you have to know who the enemy is. According to Ephesians 6:12 and James 4:7, who is the enemy? If you could see him, how would it improve your chances of overcoming him?
3. Considering the odds, reflect on what Isaiah 59:19 teaches regarding the only power by which human beings will ever overcome.
4. Why could the devil be anxious for you to focus on trying to overcome your character defects and bad behaviors?
5. Make a positive application of 2 Corinthians 3:18 as it relates to becoming more like Jesus.
6. Provide examples of how love turned "duty" into "delight."
7. List practical steps you can take to fight the good fight of faith mentioned in 1 Timothy 6:12.
8. In John 15:1-8, does Jesus command us to "bear fruit" or to "abide"? How many times does Jesus mention the words "abide" or "remain"? How would you apply this to dealing with failures in your life, or in trying to perfect a Christlike character?

CHAPTER 8

A Friend Indeed!

*O*ne evening I was sitting on the edge of my bed when my 11-year-old daughter came running excitedly into the room. In her exuberance and enthusiasm she hadn't noticed that my wire-framed glasses were sitting on the bed beside me until after she plopped down squarely upon them. With a gasp of alarm she jumped back to her feet, turned, looked down, and then burst into tears as she saw the twisted, pretzel-like state of my glasses—now minus both lenses.

"Oh, Daddy," she said through tears. "I'm so sorry, I'm so-o-o sorry! I ruined your glasses."

I assured her that all would be well and told her that I was about five years overdue in getting them replaced anyway. I pulled her in close, gave her a hug, and told her I would just get another pair, and everything would be fine.

"No, Daddy," she said, refusing to be comforted. "You don't have any money, so you won't be able to get a new pair of glasses."

I told her I had insurance, and would have to pay for only part of the expense. I promised her it was not going to be a problem. Gradually she calmed down, stopped crying, and dried her eyes. We talked a bit more, and then she went off to bed.

The next morning I was just finishing breakfast when she started out the door for school. She paused on the steps and then came back to where I was sitting and gave me a kiss. With a confident smile she said, "Daddy, Jesus is going to send you money for glasses today."

I asked her how she knew that, and she responded, "I told Him this morning how bad I felt that I had ruined your glasses. I told Him that if I had enough money, I would buy you a new pair, but that I didn't have any money. So I asked Him if He would send money for you, since I don't have any, and I know that He is going to do that, Daddy, because that's just the kind of friend Jesus is."

She dashed out the door happy and certain, and I turned to my wife to ask if we had some money we could place in an envelope and put in the mailbox. "This is not good," I said. "Jesus knows that I have insurance and that I don't need any extra money, so what is going to happen to Lindsey's faith when she finds out that her prayer isn't answered? How are we going to explain this to her without eroding her faith?"

When my wife replied, "I think He's going to do it!" I concluded that the problem was twice as big as I had thought it was. I said a prayer that God would somehow come through so *their* faith would not have to be shaken—though looking back, there is some question as to *whose* faith was shaking.

We went off to work and when I came home for lunch, I checked the mailbox. There were some letters *asking* for money, but there was no letter containing money. I returned to work wondering what we were going to do and how this whole thing was going to affect Lindsey. That night I went into Seattle, where I gave the last in a weeklong series of presentations for a Korean church. As I was leaving, they gave me a thank-you card that I left, unopened, on the dining room table.

The next day, in my own church, I was telling a small group of fellow Christians about my dilemma involving Lindsey's prayer for money. My wife, who was in the group, interrupted to ask me if I knew what was in the envelope I had left on the table the night before. I told her it was a thank-you card and asked why she wanted to know. She then informed me that it contained a $100 bill. She followed that question with a second one, asking me what *day* the money had arrived. I was forced to acknowledge that it came on the same day Lindsey had prayed as Marji smugly concluded, "Oh, Lee of little faith."

There was certainly a lesson in it for me, but the thing I most remember from the experience is an 11-year-old girl saying, "I *know* that He is going to do that, Daddy, because that's just the kind of friend Jesus is." *That's* the kind of friend Jesus is! Aren't you glad He is a friend like that?

There's an old cliché that says, "A friend in need is a friend indeed." Have you heard it? What does it mean? It means that if someone sticks by you when you are in trouble and the going is rough, you can be sure they are a true friend. Fair-weather friends disappear at the first sign of a storm, but a friend who is there for you when you are in need . . . is a friend indeed!

Proverbs 18:24 says that there is a Friend who sticks closer than a brother. I'd like to direct your thoughts to several occasions where Jesus is a friend indeed, when we are His friends in need.

Occasion 1

I need a friend like Jesus *when I realize that I am a sinner under sentence.* Why? Because Romans 6:23 says, "The wages of sin is death," and Romans 3:23 reminds us that "all have sinned, and come short of the glory of God." That means that you and I are sinners *and* that we are all living under a death sentence. That's why I need a friend like Jesus, who says in John 6:37, *"Whoever* comes to me I will never drive away" (NIV). Does "whoever" include you? Yes! Does "whoever" leave anyone out? No!

I need a friend like Jesus, who says in 1 John 1:9, "If we confess our sins, He is faithful and just to forgive our sins and to cleanse us" (NKJV). I'm thankful that Jesus doesn't stop with forgiving me! He goes further than that! He intends to cleanse me from all unrighteousness as well. He loves me too much to leave me messy. If we confess, He not only forgives; He cleanses.

And His forgiveness is *super* forgiveness. If I steal something from you and then come to you confessing that I did it, say I am sorry, and make restitution, you could choose to forgive me. If you forgive me, your forgiveness doesn't change the fact that I stole. I am still a thief, even though I am a forgiven one.

But what kind of forgiveness does Jesus offer us? In Psalm 103:12 He says, "As far as the east is from the west, so far has He removed our transgressions from us" (NKJV). How far is the east is from the west? It is an infinite distance, isn't it? In Isaiah 43:25 He says, "I am He who blots out your transgressions for My sake; and I will not remember your sins" (NKJV). Have you caught on to the kind of forgiveness Jesus is offering?

Have you ever confessed something like this to Him: "Lord, I am so sorry I did it again" (whatever "it" is)? If it is true that He remembers our sins no more, than the logical response we could expect from Him to an apology like that is "Did what again?"

Brennan Manning tells the story of a woman who came to her pastor troubled by dreams that she had been having in which Jesus appeared and conversed with her. She asked the pastor if there was any way of knowing whether these dreams were actually sent from God, or whether they were just the result of having eaten too rich a meal before bedtime.

The pastor offered her a test to try that put him somewhat at risk. He suggested that she ask "Jesus" what the last sin was that her pastor had confessed to Him. He told her that if "Jesus" gave her an answer that was correct, it would probably be conclusive evidence that it was really Jesus, since he didn't confess his sins to anyone else.

Weeks went by; then one day the woman called her pastor on the phone. "I had another dream," she said. The pastor drew a deep breath before inquiring if she had remembered to ask the test question. When she said that she had, his stomach muscles tightened and his pulse quickened, but he bravely asked her what the answer had been.

"Well," she said, "when I asked Jesus what the last sin you had confessed was, He answered, 'I can't remember.'"

"As far as the east is from the west, I will remove your sins from Me." "I will remember your sins no more." In other words, when you confess to the Lord Jesus, you are not considered a forgiven thief. You have *never been a thief*. That is *super* forgiveness, and that's a Friend indeed!

Occasion 2

When I have failed and fallen while trying to live the Christian life, I need a friend like Jesus, who inspired John to say, in 1 John 3:6,

"Whoever abides in Him does not sin" (NKJV). This text is packed with meaning that is often overlooked.

In chapter 2 we showed that "sin" or "iniquity" weren't primarily related to behavior or rules, but actually had to do with being out of relationship with Jesus—not *knowing* Him. It is not what you *do* but who you *know* that decides your eternal destiny, and this text reminds us of that fact. Consider carefully: If whoever *abides* in Him doesn't sin, then what would sin be? Sin would have to be *not abiding!* I'd like for you to consider that as our definition for sin (in a singular sense). If I am not abiding in Jesus, that is sin, regardless of how morally pure my life may be. Regardless of how much trouble I stay out of, it is sin to live my life apart from Jesus.

There are sins (plural) that are the fruits or products of not abiding in Jesus. They are things like temper, lust, or pride, which show up as symptoms of sin (singular)—not abiding. It is important, however, that we don't confuse the symptoms with the disease. If you had a tumor and the doctor treated your symptoms rather than your disease, your chances for survival would not be good. If you had measles and the doctor's treatment consisted of rubbing the spots on your skin with sandpaper, you'd seriously wonder about his skill or knowledge.

Romans 14:23 says, "Whatsoever is not of *faith* is sin." What is faith? Faith is synonymous with trust. Trust presupposes that there is a relationship involved. There are two ingredients necessary in order for trust to exist. First, you must have a person who is trustworthy. Second, you must know them well enough to trust them. If someone is completely trustworthy and I don't trust them, what is the problem? I don't know them well enough! With that in mind, how would you build faith (trust)? Do you grow faith by practicing the power of positive thinking? No! You would increase your faith by becoming better acquainted with the object of faith. Getting to know Jesus better is how you grow faith. When Paul says, "Whatsoever is not of faith is sin," he is telling us that at its heart, sin is living my life (good or bad) apart from a personal relationship with God.

Now, let's apply this to my *need* when I have experienced failure while trying to live the Christian life. I come to Jesus on the heels of my failure, and what does He say?

> "Whoever *abides* in Me sins not.
> If you are seeking to become better acquainted with Me,
> If we continue to spend quality time together,
> If you and I keep staying in touch,
> Then you are not sinning,
> Because sin is living life apart from Me."

Jesus wants us to understand that our greatest need is to *abide* (stay in contact or connection) with Him. In John 15 Jesus' last message to His disciples after a three-and-a-half-year ministry is "Abide in Me." Nine times in seven verses Jesus urges us to *abide*. I am the Vine, you are the branches. Abide in me and I in you. Unless you abide in me you will not bear fruit. Abide, ABIDE, *ABIDE!* These are His *dying words* to His disciples, His last message of instruction, given en route to Gethsemane. This is the message He is most desirous for us to remember.

What does *abide* mean? If I were to abide with you in your town, it would mean we were going to be together, stay together, spend time together, enjoy one another's company. *Abide* describes a relationship. In John 15:15 Jesus calls His disciples friends—calls *us* friends. Nevertheless, He tells these friends that they are all going to deny Him (sounds like failure and falling, doesn't it?). What does Peter say? "Not me, Lord, I'll never deny You. Everyone else may, but not me!"

Jesus says, at the end of John 13, "No, Peter, you're going to deny Me three times before the rooster crows tomorrow morning." Now for the good news! In the very next verse, in the *same conversation,* He says, "[But] Don't let your heart be troubled; [Peter;] if you believe in God, you can believe also in Me. In My Father's house, [Peter,] there are many mansions, and if that weren't true, I would have told you so. Now I'm going to prepare a place for you, [Peter,] and if I go to do that, you can be sure I'll come back for you so that where I am you can be also."

At the end of John 13 Jesus is telling Peter, "You are going to fail, Peter. You are going to blow it. You are going to disappoint yourself and Me." But right on the tail of that prediction He offers this wonderful reassurance: "Don't let your heart be troubled. . . . It's going to be all right! I'm still making a place for you, and you can count on this, Peter—I'll be coming *back* for you too. So hang in there. Abide with Me. Stay with Me, and we will have a future to share." *That* is a Friend *indeed!*

Occasion 3

When I lose a loved one to death, I need a friend like Jesus. When you lose a loved one, when you watch them take that long walk into the valley of shadows and you come back alone, you need a friend like Jesus. You need a friend like Jesus who says to Mary and Martha in John 11:23, "Your brother will rise again" (NIV).

Before the fall of the iron curtain, a Russian pastor of an underground (secret) church was arrested by the police and put in jail. While there he was interrogated regarding the names and addresses of his church members. He refused to disclose the names, even though he was threatened and tortured.

Days passed, and one afternoon they brought his 4-year-old son into the cell adjacent to his. They told the boy that if his father loved him, all he had to do was answer a few of their questions and everything would be fine. But if his father didn't love him, he would refuse to answer their questions, and the boy would suffer. They then asked the pastor once again to disclose the names of his church members. With tears streaming down his face he refused, all the while trying to reassure his son that he loved him very much.

Ruthlessly the interrogators cut off the boy's left hand, and then, as the little fellow writhed and screamed in pain, they repeated their question to his father. This horror was repeated several times, until the little boy lay dead in a pool of blood and body parts.

"Some God you serve!" sneered the police chief as he spat through the bars at the broken pastor. "I have no use for a God who would allow this sort of thing to happen." Then he and his executioners left the cell and the body, and the pastor to spend the night alone.

The pastor cried an ocean of tears as he called out from the depths of a broken heart to the God he had not denied. All at once he became aware that he was no longer alone. Someone else was in that lonely cell with him, Someone from whom light emanated. That Someone sat down on the pastor's steel cot, scooped his head up, and cradled him with strong arms against His chest. Holding that brokenhearted man against His chest, He said, "My Father sent me to tell you that He knows what it's like to watch as cruel men destroyed His precious Son. And He wanted me to tell you another thing. He also knows what it is like to be reunited forever with that same Son. *And so will you!*"

A Friend indeed! I need a friend like Jesus when I lose a loved one. A Friend who says, as He did about Lazarus so many years ago, "Our friend Lazarus sleepeth; but I go, that I may awake him out of sleep" (John 11:11).

Occasion 4

I need a friend like Jesus when I myself am dying. The truth is that if Jesus doesn't return before I reach the end of my earthly road, I too will die. So will you. Short of the Second Coming, nobody gets out alive. They say death is the one certainty, surrounded by three uncertainties: when, where, and how?

So when you come to the place where you are walking into the valley of shadows, and the things and friends of earth are growing strangely dim, you need a Friend like Jesus.

Brennan Manning tells about a new pastor who went to visit a dying man in the hospital. As he entered the man's room he jokingly pointed to an empty chair near the head of the bed and asked if the man had been expecting him. The old man replied, "No, I'm not even sure who you are."

After the pastor had introduced himself, the old man said, "Since you are a pastor, if you shut the door there I'll tell you the secret of the empty chair." He then related how, years before, a friend of his had made a suggestion that had significantly improved his prayer life. The friend had told him to place an empty chair across from himself and then imagine Jesus sitting in it, leaning forward, hands folded and elbows resting on knees, listening with interest. He had tried it and found that his prayer life was transformed into an intimate conversation with a wonderful Companion and Friend. He concluded by saying that he had been praying, in that manner, when the pastor had entered the room.

The pastor left feeling that he had received the greater blessing from their visit. A few days later the old man's daughter called to tell the pastor that her father had passed away. When the pastor asked if things had been particularly difficult at the end, the daughter replied, "Actually, he was sleeping so quietly that my husband and I decided to go get a bite to eat in the hospital cafeteria. When we came back from our meal, we discovered that Dad had died while we were gone. Apparently he had started to get out of bed," she said, "because when we found him, his head was resting on an empty chair."

I don't think the chair was empty. I believe that the Lord Jesus Christ showed up for that man, and somehow He will do the same for you and me if such a time should come before He returns—because that's just the kind of friend Jesus is. "I will never leave you nor forsake you!" He said in Hebrews 13:5 (NKJV). He will be the last to say, "Good night," and He will be the first to say, "Good morning."

Occasion 5

I will need a friend like Jesus when He finally comes back the second time. We're told that when Jesus returns to earth, one group of people will be crying for the rocks and the mountains to fall on them.

There will be another group of people, however, who will be looking eagerly toward that small cloud in the east. The sky will explode with the glory of ten thousand times ten thousand and thousands of angels. The earth will reel like a drunkard as thunder roars and lightning flashes. In the midst of that display of power and majesty, *these* people will catch a glimpse of Him who sits upon the throne. These people, who have taken John 17:3 seriously and sought to know the one true God, and Jesus Christ, whom He has sent, will find, as they gaze skyward, that they are looking into *familiar* eyes. In happy astonishment they will exclaim, "I *know* You!"

What a thrill will be theirs to see and hear Him reply, "I *know* you too! And I've come back for you, My friends! I've come back to take you home!"

Occasion 6

Finally, *I need a friend like Jesus when the high court convenes and the last judgment begins.* I used to have nightmares about that event. I would awaken terrified, in a cold sweat, just as they called my name. Even though I knew I could be forgiven, I dreaded having the whole watching universe find out *what had been forgiven.* In those nightmares I experienced the shame and embarrassment over and over. To have you know all the faults and secret failures that have peppered my life and brought disappointment to the King is a humiliation I would prefer to avoid. (My only consolation was knowing that V is toward the end of the alphabet, and most of you would have had to go first. Please don't remind me that the "first shall be last.")

But here is the good news about the final judgment. A deep voice will call my name over the public address system, and "L-E-E V-E-N-D-E-N" will echo across the cosmos. Suddenly a tall figure wearing a dazzlingly white robe will step before the throne. He will raise muscular arms with scarred hands as if to call a halt to the proceedings, and then He will say in a voice of richest music, "Father, I told Lee Venden that he didn't have to be here today. I'm standing in *for* him. He is a friend of mine, and he's already inside the city."

And the Father will reply, with a smile that can be seen for eternity, "Wonderful! Any friend of Yours is a friend of Mine! He is welcome here! I'm glad he's already home!"

That is actually what Jesus says in John 5:24: "Most assuredly, I say to you, he who heeds My word and believes in Him who sent Me has everlasting life, and shall *not come into judgment,* but has passed from death into life" (NKJV).

When you have a friend like Jesus, you don't even come up for judgment!

Yellow Roses

Can you imagine the celebration we are going to have when we all finally come home for the holidays? Can you imagine the party that will be thrown in His honor?

Henry Penn, former president of the Society of American Florists, tells of a day when two boys and a girl about 10 made a visit to his store. They wore ragged clothes, but had clean faces and hands. The boys took off their caps when they entered the shop. One of them stepped forward and said solemnly, "We're the committee, and we'd like some very nice yellow flowers."

Penn showed them some inexpensive spring flowers, but the boy said, "I think we'd like something better than that."

"Do they have to be yellow?" asked Penn.

"Yes, sir" was the reply. "Mickey would like it better if they were yellow, because he had a yellow sweater."

"Are these for a funeral?" the florist asked quietly.

The boy nodded. The girl turned to keep back the tears.

"She's his sister," the boy explained. "He was a good kid—a truck—yesterday—he was playing in the street. We saw it happen."

Then the other boy added, "Us kids took up a collection. We got 18 cents. Would roses cost an awful lot, mister? Yellow roses?"

Touched by the story of the tragedy and the loyalty and love of these youngsters, Penn replied, "I have some nice yellow roses here that I'm selling for 18 cents a dozen."

"Wow, those would be swell!" exclaimed one of the boys.

"Mickey would like those," the other one confirmed.

"I'll make up a nice bouquet," promised the sympathetic florist, "with ferns and a ribbon. Where shall I send them?"

"Would it be all right, mister, if we took 'em now?" asked one of the boys. "We'd kinda like to take 'em over and give 'em to Mickey ourselves, because ya see, mister, he was our friend, and we think he'd like it better that way."

Gratitude

In my mind's eye I can see us all gathered there beside the sea that looks like glass mingled with fire. The throne is high and lifted up. The choirs are singing, "Worthy is the Lamb that was slain." Our hearts are bursting with gratitude, and "thank you" seems hopelessly inadequate.

In the crowd a small group of us talk in broken whispers. We look for and find the angel who has the greatest access to the King. "Gabriel," we say, "we are the committee for some very nice yellow flowers. We took up a collection, and we got 18 cents. Would roses cost an awful lot, Gabriel? Yellow roses?"

Gabriel will smile in approval and understanding. "I'll make up a nice bouquet," he will say, "and have it delivered by an angel choir."

One of our group will muster his courage and ask on behalf of us all, "Would it be all right, Gabe, if we took 'em now? We'd kinda like to take 'em over and give 'em to Jesus ourselves. 'Cuz ya see, Gabe, when we were in need, He was our friend indeed, and we sorta think He'd like it better that way."

For Further Reflection

1. Reflect on a situation when a friend or loved one has been there for you in an exceptional way.
2. List ways in which Jesus has fulfilled Proverbs 18:24 for you.
3. Based upon Psalm 103:12 and Isaiah 43:25, if you were to say to God, "I'm sorry—I did it again," how would you expect Him to respond?
4. According to 1 John 2:28, what is the ultimate product of "abiding" in Jesus? What can you do to be a better abider?
5. Based on John 11:33-44, which is easier for Jesus: to facilitate new birth (conversion), or to resurrect the dead? Why?
6. Read the following series of texts, noting how Jesus disarms the power of death for His friends:
   > Hebrews 2:15
   > 1 Corinthians 15:55
   > Hebrews 13:5
   > John 11.11
7. Considering the following texts, what could you have to fear?
   > John 5:24
   > Romans 8:1
   > Romans 8:33
   > Romans 8:35-39

CHAPTER 9

Jesus: The Same Yesterday, Today, and Forever

*T*hrough sincere prayer we are brought into connection with the mind of the Infinite. We may have no remarkable evidence at the time that the face of our Redeemer is bending over us in compassion and love, but this is even so. We may not feel His visible touch, but His hand is upon us in love and pitying tenderness" (*Steps to Christ,* p. 97).

~ ~ ~

One characteristic I love most about Jesus is His concern for individuals and the particular attention He pays to details that we don't even concern ourselves with. He once pointed out that God notices if a sparrow falls to the ground, and that He has numbered the hairs on our head. As you consider Jesus in Scripture, you see this personal interest manifested over and over.

- He regularly joins the first couple for evening worship (Genesis 3).
- He personally promises a childless patriarch that he will have a son (Genesis 18).
- He stands up at Bethel to offer a fugitive hope (Genesis 28).
- He wrestles through the night to give a blessing at Jabbok (Genesis 32).
- Veiled by fire and cloud, He travels 40 years with a band of ex-slaves (1 Corinthians 10).
- He wakes up Moses and takes him home early (Jude 9).

- He hand-delivers the battle plan to Joshua, just prior to Jericho (Joshua 5).
- He takes the heat with three Hebrew boys in a fiery furnace (Daniel 3).
- He provides necessary refreshments for a wedding reception (John 2).
- He stays up late to point a Pharisee in the right direction (John 3).
- He waits at a well to offer living water to an outcast woman (John 4).
- He commends a self-conscious widow for giving two pennies to God (Mark 12).
- He stoops over a paralytic and frees him from 38 years of immobility (John 5).
- He is the Good Shepherd who leaves 99 to find one lost lamb (John 10).
- He makes a long journey to relieve the anxious heart of a Canaanite mother (Mark 7).
- He dries a widow's tears before turning her bereavement into joy (Luke 7).
- He makes a house call to a tax collector who has come up short (Luke 19).
- He heals a lecherous leper—no questions asked (Luke 7).
- He interrupts dying to provide care and a home for His widowed mother (John 19).
- He delays going home on Sunday to comfort one weeping woman (John 20).
- He shortens visiting with His Father to encourage brokenhearted Peter (Luke 24).
- He tutors two while walking toward Emmaus (Luke 24).
- He serves breakfast for seven, while heaven waits for His return (John 21).
- He refuses to take Stephen's martyrdom sitting down (Acts 7).
- He catches up with Saul on the Damascus road (Acts 9).
- He makes a Sabbath visit to an old man on Patmos (Revelation 1).

That was Jesus *yesterday,* but Hebrews 13:8 says He is "the same yesterday, and *to day,* and for ever." So how about today? Does He still show up for individuals?

Travis Allen

In January 1999 my son Kris's closest friend was diagnosed with children's leukemia. Travis and Kris had been friends since fifth grade, and their friendship had become as special as that of David and Jonathan. For years they were nearly inseparable.

Kris and I were with them at Children's Hospital in Seattle the night the Allen family learned what was causing Travis so much trouble. It was rare for someone Travis's age to get children's leukemia—so rare, in fact, that physicians traveled long distances to observe his case. When they told him what he had, they said that without treatment he would live only a few more weeks. Such news would devastate anyone, but for a 17-year-old skateboarder, it was like crashing into a concrete wall.

Travis chose to fight, and the treatments began. Radiation and chemotherapy. We had an anointing service in his hospital room, while his classmates and church friends joined in prayer back home. The pain was immense at times; Travis said it felt as if his joints were being slowly compressed in a hydraulic vise.

Tom Allen, Travis's father, teaches at the private high school that Travis attended. Trinda, his mother, is a surgical nurse at the hospital in their town. The local church and school rallied strongly in support of Travis and his family, as did his community and, via the Internet, friends from around the world. But in spite of occasional flickers of hope, Travis grew progressively worse.

Because his mother was a surgical nurse, Travis was allowed to spend part of his time at home—under her watchful supervision. Trinda was shown how to administer the special care he required and how to manage the multiple fluids carried by hoses from a backpack to a port into his heart. Though things were rough, Travis preferred to be home as much as possible. During the course of his illness, the Allens put more than 40,000 miles on their car driving between their home and the hospital.

His mother kept a faithful vigil at his bedside. At times his pain prevented much verbal communication, but it was encouraging to Travis just to know that she was there. Sometimes Trinda, who cat-napped in the chair beside his bed, would be awakened in the night to the sound of Travis whispering, "Mom, are you awake?"

On such occasions she would pray silently, *Wake me up, Lord; it's time to talk.*

Then she would listen as Travis would say, "Mom, I don't want to die at 18. I'm afraid."

Trinda would reply, "Travis, I want you to try to picture the face of Jesus. Imagine Him looking at you and smiling as He returns in glory, surrounded by angels. Try to hold that picture in your mind, Travis. Can you see Him there, in your imagination, looking into your eyes?"

"Yeah, Mom, I have the picture in my mind."

"Now just focus on His face, Travis; focus on His face." And as they contemplated Jesus together, Travis would find peace and fall back asleep.

During one hospital visit Travis asked me if it was OK to request a second anointing service. I assured him that it was always all right to ask, and we began planning the service. A couple days later, however, he took a sudden turn for the worse, and visitation was severely restricted. The second anointing was put on hold.

Days later a group of doctors came to Travis's room to give him the sad news. Their treatments and procedures were not going to help in his battle for life. Sorrowfully they told him that they didn't know how much time he had left.

Touring the Church

Things looked so grim that I was very surprised one Sunday, while helping with a work bee, to see Travis ride up to the entrance of our church. The doctors had told him that riding would cause irreversible damage to his joints, so I was especially startled to see him arrive on the BMX bicycle that had been given him by the Make-A-Wish Foundation. When I suggested he ought to be careful about his joints, he smiled and said, "That's what my mom told me as I was leaving the house, but what's she going to do to me? If I want to go to my grave with damaged joints, I guess it really doesn't make much difference."

He had come over to see how our remodeling project was progressing. "I haven't been able to be at church for a long time," he said, "but I wanted to see how the renovation is going. I've missed being here."

I told him I'd be happy to give him a personal tour, so he got off his bike and came through our doorway, walking stiffly because of pain. I showed him each area that was being remodeled, ending with our sanctuary. Travis commented enthusiastically throughout the tour. As we stood together, just below the front platform, I couldn't help wondering if the next time I saw Travis in our church he would be lying where he was then standing.

We left the sanctuary and stood talking in the foyer. Suddenly I remembered that we'd talked about a second anointing. I reminded Travis of that conversation and noted that this was the first time I'd been able to see him since we'd talked. He told me that he was still interested, and I said that I was still willing—but that I needed to ask him a question.

"Travis," I said, "do you remember the dark day when the doctors told you that you weren't going to win this battle? Well, if Jesus should choose not to heal you physically, for reasons we may not understand until we're in heaven, are you up to another disappointment?"

He tilted his head to one side, a puzzled look on his face, and then said, "I guess I didn't make it clear what I'm asking for. I'm OK with dying. Jesus and I worked that out a long time ago. I'm not asking to be healed, though if He should choose to heal me, that would be cool. I'm thinking of it more like a wedding service, or some sort of consecration service, that sorta seals the fact that I want to be His and His alone."

I was so inspired by his thinking that I replied, "Travis, other people need to hear about your confident faith and unswerving trust in Jesus. Would you feel exploited if I were to conduct an interview with you that could be taped so others could see and hear?"

"No way!" he shot back. "I'd love an opportunity to talk about

Jesus, and let me tell you, He would be the subject of any interview I'm involved with."

So I interviewed Travis. I want him to speak to you in his own words.

Interview With Travis

Travis, can you describe what it felt like to be told that you had leukemia?

I told my dad that the three worst words you could ever hear are "You have cancer"—because that means you are probably going to die.

Describe your life during the year or two prior to hearing the diagnosis. What were your goals, hopes, and dreams?

I'm a completely different person than I was a year ago! Then I lived for fun, things, and being cool. Now, simply living for fun or a good time seems like such a superficial way to live. Material possessions don't have any attraction to me now. I'd give all I ever had or will have in exchange for health. And as far as being cool is concerned, taking an open stand for Jesus is as cool as you can get.

How have your relationships with family and friends changed?

People are all that's really important. Family and friendship and time together is what counts. I like to talk about Jesus a lot. Sometimes I have even apologized to my friends for talking so much about Him that they might be thinking the conversation is sort of limited, but they always tell me it's not a problem.

Have you gotten angry with God since learning you have leukemia? Do you blame Him for your condition?

No way! He wasn't the cause of my illness. His enemy is. The devil is a jerk!

Have you not had any questions for God?

Well, I used to ask, "Why me? Why aren't all the prayers for healing being answered?" But Jesus has shown me a bigger picture, and now when I'm tempted to ask, "Why me?" I attack that question with another one. "Why not me?" Maybe there have been people with leukemia who have gotten mad at God and given up on Him. But if I can be a witness for God that demonstrates to others and to the watching universe that tragedy doesn't need to shake your trust or confidence in Him, then why not me?

Has your spiritual life changed since the diagnosis?

Yes. I love to talk about Jesus more than anything or anyone. He comforts me and strengthens me. He gives me peace in spite of my condition. I love hearing my mom read to me from the Bible and from *The Desire of Ages* about Him. Jesus is the only card I have left to play, but with that card I'll win the game.

In light of what the doctors are telling you, would you say that you now have no hope for the future?

No way! The devil can try all he wants to break me down. He can kill me, but he can't touch my eternal life.

Travis had the opportunity to repeat that lesson to his team of doctors when they came in one day for a serious discussion. They had come to talk with him about his options for "checking out." They described a number of protocols to finish off the battle he was fighting—ways in which he could be medicated and the corresponding effect on his mind or body. One of the doctors said, "Travis, in light of what we've just gone over, what do you see for your future?"

Travis answered, "Well, unless Jesus chooses to work a miracle, I'm going to be sleeping until resurrection morning. Then I will rise to meet Him. That's what I see for my future."

One of the doctors replied, "Travis, that is a wonderful concept, and I'm glad it brings you comfort."

Travis shot back, "It's not a concept, Doctor. It's in your Bible, and it's *real.*"

Just then a hospice worker came into the room with a chart and a clipboard. As she entered, one of the doctors said, "He doesn't need you. He has help far greater than any of us can give him."

I couldn't help thinking of 2 Timothy 1:12, where another spiritual giant wrote, "I know the one in whom I have put my trust, and I am sure that he is able to guard until that day what I have entrusted to him" (NRSV).

Is there a text or quotation that has come to have extra special meaning to you?

There are some verses in Psalms that have special meaning to me because they seem to be describing *my* situation. Psalm 61:1-5:

"Hear my cry, O God; listen to my prayer. From the ends of the earth I call to you, I call as my heart grows faint; lead me to the rock that is higher than I. For you have been my refuge, a strong tower against the foe. I long to dwell in your tent forever and take refuge in the shelter of your wings. For you have heard my vows, O God; you have given me the heritage of those who fear your name" (NIV). Psalm 62:1, 2: "My soul finds rest in God alone; my salvation comes from him. He alone is my rock and my salvation; he is my fortress, I will never be shaken" (NIV).

Travis's father told me of another special Bible verse. One day as he was sitting beside Travis, who was reading from the Bible, Travis suddenly said, "Dad, check this out. Matthew 22:32." Then Travis read aloud, "'I am the God of Abraham, the God of Isaac, and the God of Jacob. He is not the God of the dead but of the living'" (NIV).

"Isn't that cool, Dad?" he asked.

Tom replied that it was a neat passage, but asked Travis to explain what he found so special about it.

"Well, Dad," Travis answered, "Abraham, Isaac, and Jacob are what we call 'dead.' But Jesus says that God considers them *living*. That means that when it looks to you like I am dead, God will still consider me as living! Don't forget that, Dad. That's awesome!

What advice would you offer adults who are busily making a living?

Keep in touch with Jesus, and make the people in your life your first priority. Nothing is more important than that.

Continuing Testimonies

One evening my son and I were visiting Travis in the hospital. As he lay back against his pillows, Travis asked me how he could hang on to assurance in the light of personal failures. When I asked him what he meant, he told me that he was troubled by the fact that he sometimes had thoughts that seemed out of line for a Christian. It made him wonder, he said, whether he was really sincere about following Jesus.

I told him that those troubling thoughts were no indication that he was insincere. Paul described a similar dilemma in Romans 7 when he said he found himself doing things he didn't want to do, and not doing things that he did want to do. I told him his assurance of salvation was based not on *his* performance, but rather upon Jesus and His promise to do for us what we cannot do for ourselves.

We talked about Jesus' words in John 17:3 and how He told us that our eternal life was based upon knowing Him and His Father. I read 1 John 5:11, 12 to him, noting that *he had* a relationship with Jesus, which meant he "had the Son" and therefore eternal life as well. I reminded Travis that in spite of his troubling thoughts, he continued to seek Jesus day by day, which is all any of us can really do. Finally, we considered God's promise in Philippians 1:6, that "he who began a good work in you will carry it on to completion until the day of Christ Jesus" (NIV).

"Travis," I said, "you don't clean up your life to come to Jesus. You come to Jesus to have your life cleaned up. It's not about what you *do;* it's about who you *know.* It's not about what you *think;* it's about who you are *becoming acquainted with.*"

I will never forget the way Travis's face brightened as the Holy Spirit put it all together for him. He sat in silence for a short time, then, leaning toward me with a huge smile on his face, he said, "That's awesome! If you focus on yourself you will always feel un-certain, but if you focus on Jesus, you can be sure that *everything will be all right!*"

On another evening when we were together, Travis told me about the "night light." He told me how he would pray each night before trying to get some sleep. After committing his life anew to God, he would always ask if God would give him some indication that his prayer had gotten through. "Then the most amazing thing happens," he said. "As I lie there in bed, it is as though I am in a dark, dark cave. Then, far away in the darkness, it is as if a little glim-mer of light begins to grow. As it continues to grow, it gets closer and closer until it seems to envelope me. When that happens, I feel a warm sense of peace, and shortly after that I fall asleep."

The experience he'd described seemed so wonderful that I was left without words. Finally Travis broke the silence with a question. "Isn't that cool?" he said.

"Yes, Travis," I replied. "That is *really* cool! It reminds me of the passage in John 1:5, where it says that the Light shone in the darkness and the darkness could not overcome it."

Second Anointing

Events conspired against our being able to do a second anointing for Travis . . . until September 30, 1999. On a Thursday afternoon, Travis had to return to the hospital. He was in so much pain that hearing him cry out was unnerving to the other patients on the oncology ward, so this time he was placed in a soundproof room.

His father called my office to tell me that Travis's pain was so great that an anesthesiologist had actually had to put Travis under. "I don't want him to have to revive to such excruciating pain," Tom said. "I may have spoken with my son for the last time."

I suddenly remembered promising Travis that we would do that second anointing. "Tom," I said, "what are we going to do? I haven't been able to have the second anointing Travis asked for, and it was supposed to be a sort of wedding-like commitment service. If Travis is unconscious, how can we have a wedding without the groom being present?"

Tom said, "Let's do it anyway. He can find out in heaven that we honored his request."

I got off the phone and immediately called the administration office of the private high school Travis attended. I asked if the students could be freed from their classes in order to offer special prayer for Travis in our church, which was just across the street from the school. It was granted, and an announcement was made over the intercom. I then called the leaders of our church prayer chain and asked if they'd start calling our members to pray for Travis. After that, I got Bill Roberts, Travis's Bible teacher, and we headed for the hospital in Seattle.

When we arrived, we were directed to the soundproof room where Travis lay unconscious. As I stood at the foot of his bed, I felt sick that Travis wouldn't be aware of the anointing. I asked if we could have an extra prayer before we began the consecration service. In prayer I asked that God would somehow make it possible for Travis to know what was happening, and that He would drive the enemy out of that room long enough for Travis's request to be honored. When I looked up from that prayer, Travis was looking at me. Smiling, he said, "Thanks for coming."

I told him about the special season of prayer that his classmates and church family were having on his behalf. He smiled again and said, "That's awesome."

His parents knelt on one side of the bed, while the Bible teacher and I knelt on the other. As I began to pray, I began to feel overwhelmed by the courage of this 18-year-old. My prayer was interrupted by my tears. Suddenly I felt a hand massaging my neck and shoulders. I looked up to discover that Travis was comforting both me and his father, as if to say, "It's going to be OK, guys. It's going to be all right. We're talking to the right Person."

We finished praying, and then Travis joined in as we sang "It Is Well With My Soul." After singing, he asked us to thank all who had gathered to pray on his behalf. As I looked at him lying in that bed, I said, "Travis, you have fought a good fight. You have nearly finished the race. And when you finish, you will be crossing the finish line into a golden city."

He replied, "And I will kneel at His feet. And I will look up into the beautiful face of Jesus. I will throw my crown down before Him, and I would gladly go bald for Him again, if it would help to bring Him glory!"

Final Testimonies

The pain backed off, and Travis was able to return home for a while. On October 14 my neighbor and his daughter went to visit. Travis told them he was living on borrowed time. In response, my neighbor asked, "Are you surprised when you wake up in the morning and find that you are still here?"

"Not really," Travis replied. "But I won't be surprised if one day I wake up and find that I am looking into the face of Jesus. That won't be a surprise either."

On October 24 Trinda Allen called our home for my son Kris. She told him that Travis was feeling a bit stronger and wanted to get out of the house. She asked if Kris would like to come along and push the wheelchair as they took Travis to the mall. After a day together they sat and talked in Travis's room until finally Travis said, "I'm real tired, Kris. Let's pick up tomorrow where we've left off. Right now, I think I just need to go to sleep."

Early the following morning Travis woke his parents and told them he needed to get to Children's Hospital quickly. They all sensed the urgency and hustled him out to the car. As they headed into rush-hour traffic, Travis told them he thought this would be their last trip to the hospital. He said he was at peace.

Unknown to Travis, his blood had become so thin that his veins and arteries were no longer able to contain it. Fluids had begun to seep into his body cavity, and the pressure was causing him to feel as if he urgently needed to use the bathroom. The hospital was still more than 30 miles away, so in response to his request, they pulled off the highway at the next available place. They drove into the parking lot of a Denny's Restaurant, where they helped Travis out of the car. As they entered the restaurant, the hostess asked if they would like a table for three. Then suddenly she said, "Are you OK, son?"

They told her they needed a restroom, and she pointed the way to a tiny, two-stall restroom at the end of an aisle. Trinda stood watch at the door to prevent anyone from entering as Tom helped Travis inside. No one was in the restroom, and both stall doors stood open. Tom chose the handicapped stall because it was larger. As he was trying to help Travis get situated, he suddenly noticed under the divider the trousers and shoes of someone standing in the next stall. For a moment he resented the fact that anyone else would be in the room while Travis was in such critical condition, but he soon forgot about it as he turned his attention back to Travis.

Travis asked for his mom, and Tom called for Trinda to join them. She came in and began asking Travis to describe what he was feeling. "I can't breathe," he said.

At that moment the man in the stall next to them spoke. "You're going to be OK, Travis," he said.

Travis asked his father to call 911, and Tom rushed out of the restroom to do so. While Tom was out of the room, Travis told his mother, "I think I'm dying."

The man in the next stall immediately responded by saying, "You're going to be fine, Travis. I am here." Trinda told her son to listen to what the man was saying.

In less than five minutes an ambulance arrived from a nearby hospital, and Tom led the paramedics into the restroom. The team quickly laid Travis on a stretcher while his mom knelt beside his head. As they were working, the man from the next stall came out, moved around Tom, and knelt across from Trinda at Travis's head, where he continued telling Travis that everything was going to be all right.

The lead paramedic asked the man if he was Travis's father. "No," he replied. "I am his friend." He stayed by as the stretcher was being carried out, assuring Travis that everything was going to be fine. Travis slipped into unconsciousness as the man helped slide the stretcher into the ambulance. Though the ambulance report mentions that they were assisted by a stranger, nobody got his name or noted when he left.

They transported Travis to a nearby Flight-for-Life helicopter and headed for Children's Hospital. Tom and Trinda got into their car and headed through the rush-hour traffic, miraculously beating the helicopter to the hospital. They were there as he came into the ER. They were holding him when his heart monitor went flat.

Just then, thunder shook the hospital as a cloudburst unleashed torrential rain. The helicopter pilot ran back in, saying, "I'm sure not going to try to take off in that!"

An ER nurse replied, "I guess not! You would probably run into God!"

In my imagination I love to replay this scene. Travis is being carried out of that Denny's Restaurant looking into the face of Someone who is saying, "You're going to be fine, Travis. Everything is going to be OK."

It seems but a moment later that Travis blinks, and as he opens his eyes, he says to himself, "He's right! I do feel fine. Everything does seem to be OK!" Then suddenly he realizes that the face he's looking into is shining with glory.

He hears an angel say, "Travis, there was a little change. Your last thought was that you were being taken to the hospital on the Flight-for-Life copter, but actually, Travis, it is the Resurrection morning, and this is the Flight-for-Eternal-Life! You're being taken home. Jesus has come for His friends, and you are one of them!"

~ ~ ~

"The Elder Brother of our race is by the eternal throne. He looks upon every soul who is turning his face toward Him as the Savior. . . . He is watching over you, trembling child of God. Are you tempted? He will deliver. Are you weak? He will strengthen. Are you ignorant? He will enlighten. Are you wounded? He will heal. . . . 'Come unto me' is His invitation" (*The Desire of Ages,* p. 329).

For Further Reflection
1. What personal encouragement do you find in considering Luke 12:6, 7 and Matthew 10:29-31? Why would Jesus tell you that God counts hairs?
2. Read Daniel 3:13-25. In what ways has Jesus "taken the heat" with you?
3. Read John 4:7-29. Why do you suppose this woman came clear out of town to get water? Why was she startled that Jesus would talk to her? Where do you see yourself in this story?
4. Read Luke 19:1-10. Give reasons Zacchaeus was surprised to be noticed by Jesus. What sort of encouragement do you find in verse 7?
5. Read John 20:1-18. First, try to imagine what is going on in heaven at the time this story takes place. Next, reflect on reasons Jesus had to be eager to head for home. Finally, consider what His delay means for you.
6. What are some of the changeless characteristics of Jesus that mean the most to you?
7. Because it is likely that words will fail you when you finally meet Jesus face to face, write out a thank-you note to Him now.

Favorite "Jesus" Books

Badenas, Robert	*Meet Jesus*
Bishop, Jim	*The Day Christ Died*
Bishop, Jim	*The Day Christ Was Born*
Blanco, Jack	*The Clear Word*
Card, Michael	*Immanuel*★
Christ, Jesus	*Holy Bible*
Field, Kenneth	*Him*★ (available online at http//www.more aboutjesus.org)
Hardinge, Leslie	*These Watched Him Die*
Holmes, Marjorie	*Two From Galilee*
Ireland, Joan Krogstad	*My Beloved Son*
Johnson, Kim Allen	*The Gift*
Johnson, Kim Allen	*The Morning*
Keller, Phillip	*Rabboni*
Lewis, C. S.	*The Lion, the Witch, and the Wardrobe*
Lucado, Max	*Six Hours One Friday*
Manning, Brennan	*The Boy Who Cried Abba*
Marchiano, Bruce	*Jesus, Yesterday, Today and Forever*★
Marchiano, Bruce	*In the Footsteps of Jesus*
Miller, Calvin	*The Book of Jesus*
Miller, Calvin	*The Singer*★ (The Singer Trilogy)
Oursler, Fulton	*The Greatest Story Ever Told*★
Oursler, April	*The Tales Christ Told*
Pelser, Frederick	*Man of Galilee*
Peterson, Eugene	*Message*
Portvliet, Rien	*He Was One of Us*

Rasi, H. M.	*The Life of Jesus*
Rasmussen, Robert	*Imagine Meeting Him*★
Roddy, Lee	*Jesus*
Thomas, Mack	*Through the Eyes of Jesus*
Venden, Morris	*It's Who You Know*
Venden, Morris	*How Jesus Treated People*
Venden, Morris	*The Answer Is Prayer*
Venden, Morris	*How to Make Christianity Real*
Venden, Lee	*The Pleasure of His Company*
White, Ellen	*The Story of Redemption*
White, Ellen	*Steps to Christ*
White, Ellen	*Thoughts From the Mount of Blessing*
White, Ellen	*Positive Christian Living (Christ's Object Lessons)*
White, Ellen	*The Story of Jesus* (for boys and girls)
White, Ellen	*The Desire of Ages*★
Zondervan	*The Amplified Bible*

★Personal favorites.

Favorite "Jesus" Videos

Jesus of Nazareth
Matthew
The Greatest Story Ever Told

More About Jesus
BIBLE STUDY GUIDES

*I*f you enjoyed this book by Lee Venden, then you'll want to visit his Web site and download the free lessons about a relationship with Jesus. Just go to www.MoreAboutJesus.org and click on "Interactive Lessons."

Jesus is the theme of these relational lessons that illustrate how a personal friendship with Jesus is the sum and substance of Christian life. Each lesson lifts Jesus up and provides clear, practical instruction on how to develop a meaningful relationship with Him.

Beginning with a humorous lead-in, each lesson then moves to a key thought and theme before introducing a page and a half of interactive thought questions, salted with occasional illustrations and gentle prods to stimulate thinking. The first seven lessons are focused on developing a personal relationship with Jesus; the last six show how Jesus and knowing Him are the central core of Bible doctrines.